LAW FOR LIBRARIANS

A handbook for librarians in England and Wales

LAW FOR LIBRARIANS

A handbook for librarians in England and Wales

Ian McLeod LL B BA
Solicitor, Senior Lecturer in Law, City of London Polytechnic

and

Penelope Cooling LL B
Solicitor, formerly Lecturer in Law, Leicester Polytechnic

THE LIBRARY ASSOCIATION · LONDON
A Clive Bingley Book

© Ian McLeod and Penelope Cooling 1990

Published by
Library Association Publishing Ltd
7 Ridgmount Street
London WC1E 7AE

First published 1990

British Library Cataloguing in Publication Data

McLeod, Ian
  Law for librarians : Ian McLeod, Penelope Cooling.
  1. Great Britain. Law
  I. Title   II. Cooling, Penelope
  344.1

  ISBN 0-85157-449-1

While the information contained in this book is believed to be accurate as at the end of November 1989, neither the authors nor the publisher can accept any legal responsibility or liability for any errors or omissions.

164 7 104566 1201

Typeset from authors' disk in 10/11pt Times by Library Association Publishing Ltd
Printed and made in Great Britain by Billing & Sons Ltd, Worcester

Contents

Introduction

In every work regard the writer's end,
For none can compass more than they intend.
                    (Alexander Pope, *An essay on criticism.*)

We have written this book to help librarians to increase their awareness of the legal context within which they work.

Throughout the book we have tried to make the material accessible through clarity of exposition rather than through dilution of content. We have made the fundamental assumption that the reader begins with no legal education whatsoever. Two specific consequences of this assumption are the inclusion of a chapter dealing with the framework of the English legal system, and the provision of an Appendix outlining both the citation and use of legal sources, and the conventional abbreviations of judges' titles.

Rather less fundamentally we have assumed that the typical reader will be working in the public library service, although we hope that most of the book will be of use to all librarians, no matter who their employer is.

The all-pervasive nature of law presented us with difficult problems as to where to draw the line between inclusion and exclusion, in view of the practical necessity of keeping the scale of the book under control. For example, in chapter 3 we consider the law of libel in some depth, whereas we have omitted the tort of injurious falsehood, which imposes liability on the originator of falsehoods if they are maliciously published and are not only calculated to produce, but also actually do produce, damage. The difference from our point of view seems to be purely practical: defamation actually operates as a major constraint on freedom of speech, whereas injurious falsehood is seldom encountered outside the pages of legal textbooks.

Also, drawing on our experience of advising members of a variety of other professions during our careers in local government, we have attempted to distinguish between those matters − such as copyright − in respect of which we have tried to develop the sort of legally informed awareness which a professional librarian might reasonably be expected to possess, and those matters − such as dismissal of staff − in respect of which it might be reasonable to expect a librarian to consult his employer or his employer's solicitors. In this context, the material in chapter 5 on data protection caused us the greatest difficulty. We are confident that most, if not all, librarians' employers will already have provided full briefing papers on the practical implications of the relevant aspects of the legislation, which probably makes any comment of ours superfluous. Nevertheless we felt that some treatment of the topic was required in this book. Accordingly, we have tried to provide an overview of the legal aspects of the topic, without making any attempt to provide a fully comprehensive treatment, which would be beyond the scope of this book in any event.

At all times, the reader is urged to remember not only that this book, covering a vast range of law in a relatively small compass, has been written for non-lawyers but also that the law can change rapidly. It follows from this that we have not been able to cover all the nuances of the law in all respects, and that, since books usually have a lifespan of several years, any law book may be out-of-date in some respects by the time it is being read. More importantly, at a practical level, any reader who is confronted with a real legal problem should ensure that he obtains legal advice. If by writing this book we have added to the ranks of 'barrack room lawyers' we shall have done a disservice to all concerned.

The current state of affairs in local government is, of course, such that some degree of privatization may seem to be a real possibility in the relatively near future. We have not attempted any serious coverage of the problems which this might create in a library context, because these will essentially involve questions of the interpretation of the relevant statutory provisions if and when they are passed. However, we have mentioned those provisions of the Local Government and Housing Act 1989 which relate to companies in which local authorities are interested.

When citing cases, we have given only the date in the body of the text, with references to law reports being relegated to an Appendix. In the Appendix we have favoured the citation of the All England Law Reports where they contain the case in question, because we think this is probably the most widely available series of Reports. However, readers lacking access to the All England Law Reports, but having access to other series, may well find the cases reported elsewhere. When looking in other series, it is important to note that the inevitable delay in editing, printing and distributing law reports means that the precise year of the volume in which a report appears might vary slightly from one series to another.

We have discussed the law of England and Wales. This is conventionally referred to as *English* law, merely as a form of shorthand and without any disrespect being intended to natives of the Principality. Readers outside England and Wales should proceed with caution. English law, in common with the law of every other country, does not travel well, and many of the principles we have discussed may not apply even as close to home as Scotland, let alone other places further afield.

We have consistently referred to librarians as if they are all male. This is simply a matter of convention and convenience. If pressed on the matter, we would seek to rely on the presumption used in relation to the interpretation of Acts of Parliament, and contained in s. 6 of the Interpretation Act 1978, namely that words importing the masculine gender include the feminine.

We are grateful to John Sumsion, Esq., the Registrar of Public Lending Right, for enhancing our awareness of the way in which P.L.R. operates, and to Her Majesty's Stationery Office for permission to reproduce Forms A and B in Chapter 6. Above all, however, we are grateful to our publishers for having sufficient confidence in the project to enable it to proceed, and more particularly to Barbara Jover and Lin Franklin for their exemplary patience throughout.

We have each written individual chapters, but we have also revised each other's work. Convention therefore requires each of us publicly to accept responsibility for the whole, although if any errors are drawn to our attention we shall no doubt privately blame each other.

Ian McLeod
November 1989   Penelope Cooling

1 An introduction to the English legal system

1.1.01 Before dealing with individual aspects of law which are of interest to librarians, it is necessary to sketch an outline of the English legal system as a whole. The purpose of this chapter, therefore, is to provide such a sketch in order to provide an overall context within which specific topics may be placed, and to explain some of the technical terminology which will inevitably be encountered from time to time.

1.1.02 One point which will be apparent throughout this book is that lawyers are very keen on analysis and classification, so it is appropriate to begin with the different ways of classifying the whole subject area which is usually, if rather simplistically, merely referred to as *law*.

CLASSIFICATIONS OF LAW

1.2.01 Unfortunately, some of the most basic terms used in legal classifications have a variety of meanings, depending on the context in which they are used. However, it is possible to deal fairly briefly with most of the major variations.

The possible meanings of *common law*

1.2.02 The phrase *common law* can be contrasted with *statute law*, *equity* and *civil law*.

Common law and statute law

1.2.03 When common law is contrasted with statute law, it means that part of law which is contained in the decisions of the courts, rather than having been enacted by Parliament. The explanation of the use of the word *common* in this context is historical. In the centuries after the Norman Conquest, the King's judges travelled round the country deciding cases in various places. This meant that the judges built up an overall

1

picture of the law in various areas, and by extending the area of operation of sensible principles and allowing less sensible ones to lapse, they were able to unify the law of the entire country. Another way of saying that the law was unified was to say that it was common to the whole country, and so it was called the *common law*.

Common law and equity

1.2.04 The heart of the common law was originally the writ system. Writs were − and still are − documents issued in order to start an action in the courts. The court office which issued writs was called the chancery, and its head was the Lord Chancellor. In the early stages, the common law was flexible and responded to new situations as they arose by issuing new forms of writ. In the fourteenth century the common law became more rigid. The attitude of the office of chancery came to be that if a potential litigant asked for a writ, and there was no existing form to cover the facts which he alleged, this could only be because he had no right capable of legal protection.

1.2.05 Even in those cases where the common law was willing to provide an appropriate writ, an additional problem could arise. If a case was proved by evidence, the courts would regard themselves as being bound to make the order for which the proceedings had been brought. Normally this would be unobjectionable, but sometimes it would cause injustice.

1.2.06 Take for example a case where there was written evidence of a debt, but the debtor repaid the money without ensuring that the documentary evidence was cancelled by his creditor. In these circumstances, if the creditor sued the debtor alleging non-payment, the courts would say 'what better evidence could we have that the debt remains outstanding than the uncancelled document which the creditor has produced to us?' Accordingly the courts would order the debtor to repay the money, even though he had already done so once. To be fair to the courts, it must be emphasized that they were not saying that double repayment was just. What they were saying was that the overriding principle was that disputes should be decided according to the best evidence which could be produced, and in this case the best evidence was the uncancelled document.

1.2.07 This combination of general stagnation and individual injustice gave rise to the emergence of *equity*. What happened was that litigants who were unable to obtain satisfaction from the King's courts developed the practice of petitioning the King himself, asking for an exception from the general rules to be made in their cases. Before deciding what to do about individual petitions, the King would take advice. One of his principal advisers was the Lord Chancellor, who not only had expert knowledge of the common law through his headship of the office of chancery, but also, at this stage of legal history, was perceived as having the additional advantage of being a clergyman. This latter qualification meant that he could be presumed to have an informed conscience as to what ought to be done. It was for this reason that the Lord Chancellor was often called 'the keeper of the King's conscience'.

1.2.08 Although the King originally made his own decisions in the light of advice which he received, he soon developed the practice of delegating to the Lord Chancellor the whole of the task of making decisions on individual petitions. As this became established practice, petitions began to be presented directly to the Lord Chancellor, by-passing the King altogether. In the initial stages the Lord Chancellor issued decrees in the King's name. By the end of the fifteenth century he was issuing them in his own name. Thus the *office* of chancery had evolved into the *court* of chancery.

1.2.09 Although the existence of the court of chancery alongside the courts of common law had real advantages for the development of the law and the working of justice in individual cases, it also gave rise to the possibility of conflict when two courts − one of chancery and one of common law − made conflicting orders in relation to the same facts. The details of the way in which this conflict was resolved is a fascinating piece of legal history. Briefly, however, in the early part of the seventeenth century it became established that where equity and the law conflict, equity prevails. Furthermore, the introduction of the Judicature Acts 1873−5 merged the administration of the systems of law and equity, laying the foundations of the present arrangement whereby both systems are applied by the same courts.

1.2.10 The fact that equity is a system of principle rather than a vehicle for the caprice of individual judges can be conveniently illustrated by the case of *Paton v. British Pregnancy Advisory Service* (1978). The case raised the question of whether an injunction was an appropriate remedy, so before looking at the facts it is necessary to note two points. First, an injunction is an order of the court telling someone to do, or not to do, some specified act. Secondly, injunctions are equitable in origin.

1.2.11 The facts of *Paton* were that a woman wanted to have an abortion. Her husband, who was also the father of the child in the womb, did not agree. He asked the court for an injunction to prevent his wife from having an abortion. (An injunction is an equitable remedy, which, in the event of non-compliance, is itself enforceable by committal to prison for contempt of court.) Sir George Baker P. decided that the case really came down to whether the father had any legal rights in the matter, in which context he said:

I ask the question, 'If an injunction were ordered, what could be the remedy?' and I do not think I need say any more than that no judge could even consider sending a husband or wife to prison for breaking such an order. That of itself seems to me to cover the application here; this husband cannot by law stop his wife by injunction from having what is . . . a lawful abortion.

Common law and civil law

1.2.12   Another way in which the phrase *common law* is used is by way of contrast to *civil law*. In this context, the distinction which is being drawn is basically between the English legal system (together with those countries whose legal systems are derived from it, such as Australia, New Zealand and the United States of America) on the one hand and the legal systems of most of the states of Western Europe on the other.

1.2.13   The historical origin of this distinction is that continental Europe was heavily influenced by Roman Law, and the modern European systems still show this heritage to a marked degree. In England, on the other hand, Roman Law and its concepts have had no lasting impact. One of the most important aspects of the distinction is that the basic principles of law in a civil law country will be found in an enactment, or a series of enactments, called a code whereas in a common law country the basic principles will have evolved through the decisions of the courts. Admittedly, as the rate of social change has accelerated, statute law has overtaken the common law as the main vehicle of legal change even in common law countries, but the historical perspective continues to influence the way in which lawyers from different traditions approach what are basically similar problems. An unfortunate terminological confusion also arises when dealing with codification, because even in the English legal system some comprehensive statutes are referred to as being codes, but all this means is that, when enacted, they contained all the English law on the topic concerned. The fundamental point remains that much of the basis of English Law emerged piecemeal over the centuries as and when suitable cases came before the courts, rather than being formulated as a coherent whole.

1.2.14   It is worth noting that because Wales became politically unified with England at an early stage, it is part of the English legal system, and generally the same law applies throughout England and Wales. By way of contrast, Scotland, having retained its political independence for rather longer, and having previously been a civil law country, now finds itself with a curiously hybrid system, which many Scots lawyers regard as being the best of both the common law and civil law worlds. Northern Ireland is basically a common law jurisdiction, but for a variety of reasons it is not unusual to find that some statutes apply only to that Province, and that others do not apply there.

Other possible meanings of *civil law*

1.2.15 Quite apart from its use in contradistinction to *common law*, the phrase *civil law* does have distinct and proper usages even within the English legal system. The alternatives to *civil law* are variously *criminal law*, *ecclesiastical* (or *canon*) *law*, and *military law*. Only the distinction between *civil law* and *criminal law* need be considered here, since the affairs of neither the Church nor the armed forces are within the scope of this book.

Civil law and *criminal law*

1.2.16 The dividing line between civil law and criminal law is best approached from an historical perspective. The essence of the distinction is that in civil law (involving, among other things, breach of contract, and torts such as libel, slander and negligence), the focus is on compensating the victim, whereas in criminal law (involving matters such as theft and murder), the focus is on punishing the offender.

1.2.17 Closer examination of the relevant law shows that this version of the distinction, although a useful starting point, is something of an overstatement. This is so partly because, in modern times, the range of powers available to the courts exercising criminal jurisdiction has increased substantially, with some possible options (such as probation) being intended to help the offender rather than to punish him. What is more, quite apart from such rehabilitative possibilities, there are circumstances in which a court can compensate the victim of crime at the same time as it sentences the offender.

1.2.18 Similarly, there are circumstances in which the court in a civil case can award damages over and above the sum required for compensation, with the intention of punishing the wrongdoer [paras. 1.6.08 *et seq*.]. Nevertheless, the basic point remains that in a criminal case, once guilt has been proved, the fundamental question is 'what should be done with the offender?' whereas in a civil case the corresponding question, on proof of liability, is 'what should be done for the victim?'

1.2.19 The most immediately apparent distinction between *civil law* and *criminal law* lies in the basic terminology. A typical civil case will be called an *action*, and will be concerned with proof of *liability*. This terminology is actually only one of a number of possibilities, which vary according to the nature of the case, but a complete list would be tedious. A criminal case will be called a *prosecution* and will be concerned with proof of *guilt*. The legal description of the parties also varies. In a typical civil case a *plaintiff sues* a *defendant*. In a criminal case a *prosecutor prosecutes* the other party, who may be called either the *defendant*, the *accused*, or even, if he is in custody, the *prisoner*.

1.2.20 Secondly, the standard of proof differs between civil and

5

criminal cases. A plaintiff need prove his case only on the balance of probabilities, but a prosecutor must prove his case beyond reasonable doubt. The balance of probabilities test merely means that the plaintiff must show that it is more likely than not that what he alleges to have happened actually did happen. Proof beyond reasonable doubt involves a far higher standard, and therefore requires evidence of far greater cogency.

1.2.21 Finally, there are various other distinctions between civil and criminal cases, including detailed matters of procedure, evidence, costs, and legal aid.

Public law and private law

1.2.22 The importance of the distinction between *public law* and *private law* came to prominence during the 1980s, largely as a result of certain technical changes to the procedure by which cases are brought in the High Court. It is difficult to be absolutely precise as to where the line is drawn, but a useful perspective can be derived from the fact that some areas of law involve public bodies or public officials doing things which, by their very nature, could not be done by private individuals. Where this is so, the concept of public law becomes relevant.

1.2.23 For example, if a local authority builds some houses on land which it does not own, they will be liable in tort on the grounds of trespass, just as anyone else would be: their status as a public body is irrelevant. The position is different if a local authority issues an enforcement notice in respect of a piece of development which has been undertaken without planning permission. In this case, the action taken by the local authority is being taken only because they are a local authority: no private individual could have taken the enforcement action. In other words, the trespass example falls within the sphere of private law, and the planning example falls within the sphere of public law.

1.2.24 The courts are still very actively expanding the idea of public law, which means that at the present stage of legal development it is impossible to indicate with any great accuracy exactly where the boundaries are to be drawn.

1.2.25 The precise significance of the distinction between public law and private law will depend on all the circumstances of a particular case, but two general points can usefully be made.

1.2.26 First, a court which is considering a challenge to a matter which is governed by public law will tend to supervise the manner in which the matter was dealt with, rather than imposing its own view as to what the outcome should have been. In other words the court acknowledges that some kinds of decision − such as whether a local authority wishes to take enforcement action against unauthorized development, for example – are properly within the discretion of the public decision-makers themselves, because such decisions are inextricably linked with questions of policy and subjective assessments of the merits of the situation. In cases such as these, the court will compel the public decision-maker to consider each matter individually and in a fair way, having regard to all legally relevant factors. However, provided the *decision-making process* is unimpeachable, the *actual decision* is not something with which the court will interfere.

1.2.27 Secondly, certain aspects of procedure apply only to public law cases. These are thought to be necessary to protect public decision-makers from the constant risk of petty, vexatious and frivolous challenges made by people wanting to use the judicial process as a means of making political points. One of the most important of these safeguards is that no private individual has the right to challenge a matter of public law without first making a preliminary application to the court, in which he asks for leave to make the full application.

Substantive law and procedural law

1.2.28 Some rules of law deal with substantive rights and duties, whilst others deal with the procedural aspects of enforcing the substantive rules.

1.2.29 When a judge draws a distinction between matters of substance and matters of procedure, he will usually say why, in the context in question, the distinction is relevant. No exhaustive catalogue can be given here, but by way of example it can be said that time limits are often – though not always – procedural. The significance of a time limit being held to be procedural is well illustrated by the case of *Kammins Ballrooms Co. Ltd. v. Zenith Investments Ltd.* (1970), which is examined in detail in paras. 1.5.15 *et seq.*, in the context of statutory interpretation.

1.2.30 An example of a substantive time limit will be found in s. 21 of the Firearms Act 1968, under which it is an offence for any person to possess a firearm or ammunition within five years of his release from certain types of custodial sentences. Here the time limit is clearly part of the substance of the offence.

Classification by subject-matter

1.2.31 The classifications which have been outlined are all basic, in the sense that they are part of the conceptual structure of the legal system. However, the classifications which are referred to most frequently are those which are formulated according to the subject-matter under consideration. As a matter of convenience, most lawyers think of an identifiable body of law dealing with contract, another one dealing with tort, and so on. These usages may be convenient shorthand, but in reality there are so many overlaps that any attempt to force material to fit such

7

a pre-determined scheme will result in a seriously blinkered approach, leading to errors of oversight, at the very least.

THE HIERARCHY OF THE COURTS

1.3.01 The hierarchy of the courts can be represented, in outline, as follows:

European Court of Justice

House of Lords   Judicial Committee of
                                                  the Privy Council

Court of Appeal

High Court

Crown Court   County Court

Magistrates' Court   Administrative
                                                  Tribunals and
                                                  Statutory Inquiries

The jurisdiction of the principal courts

1.3.02 The European Court of Justice is the court of the European Communities. Its jurisdiction covers matters of Community Law, such as relationships between member states, as well as cases which are referred to it by the courts of member states on the basis that a matter of European Law is involved. In this second category of case, the decision of the European Court will be binding on the courts of the member states. (The relationship between English law and Community law is considered further in paras. 1.7.01 *et seq.*)

1.3.03 The traditional status of the House of Lords, which is more formally known as the Judicial Committee of the House of Lords, was that of the highest court of appeal in the English legal system. Subject to what has been said about the European Court of Justice, this remains true. The jurisdiction of the House of Lords covers both civil and criminal cases.

1.3.04 The Judicial Committee of the Privy Council, which is usually known simply as the Privy Council, stands outside the main hierarchy of the courts. It has a wide-ranging jurisdiction, including appeals from some Commonwealth countries, certain Admiralty and ecclesiastical matters, and appeals arising from a variety of professional disciplinary tribunals, such as those dealing with doctors, dentists and opticians. The

Judicial Committee of the Privy Council usually consists of members who also sit in the Judicial Committee of the House of Lords, although in practice (as the outline diagram suggests) the phrase 'judicial committee' is used even less frequently in relation to the House of Lords than it is in relation to the Privy Council.

1.3.05 The Court of Appeal is organized into two Divisions, one with civil and one with criminal jurisdiction.

1.3.06 The High Court has both civil and criminal jurisdiction. It is largely a court of first instance − in other words it actually tries cases, rather than merely hearing appeals from other courts − but it does also have some supervisory and appellate jurisdiction. Its criminal jurisdiction is almost entirely confined to supervisory and appellate matters.

1.3.07 The Crown Court has both civil and criminal jurisdiction. The former is almost entirely concerned with appeals from the magistrates' courts, but the latter extends to trials as well as to appeals.

1.3.08 The County Court has an exclusively civil jurisdiction, which makes it unique among the principal courts of the English legal system. Its jurisdiction is generally limited according to the value of the claim. For example, in claims arising out of contract and tort, the current limit is £5,000. One important aspect of the County Court's jurisdiction concerns matters of matrimonial law, such as divorce.

1.3.09 The Magistrates' Courts have an enormously wide jurisdiction covering both criminal law and certain aspects of civil law, excluding contract and tort.

1.3.10 As their names suggest, administrative tribunals and statutory inquiries are not courts and therefore cannot be part of the hierachy of the courts. Nevertheless, they are generally subject to control by the courts, by way of either appeal or supervisory review. A major difference between tribunals and courts is that the members of a tribunal will usually have extensive, practical knowledge of the type of cases which come before them. Additionally, tribunals tend to be less formal, cheaper and generally more accessible than courts. Examples of tribunals include Industrial Tribunals, dealing with certain types of disputes between employers and employees, and Social Security Appeal Tribunals, whose jursidiction is self-evident.

1.3.11 Inquiries are also usually conducted by people with technical expertise. They also tend to be less formal, cheaper and more accessible than the courts. Nevertheless, they are essentially different from tribunals, as indicated by the following comment from the Council on Tribunals Annual Report for 1960:

Tribunals, generally speaking, exercise an independent jurisdiction: they decide particular cases by applying rules and regulations and sometimes by using their own discretion. Inquiries, on the other

9

hand, form part of the process by which a Minister exercises his discretion — discretion for which he is answerable to Parliament.

Examples of inquiries include appeals to the Secretary of State for the Environment against the refusal of planning permission by a local authority.

Rights of appeal

1.3.12   There is no single, coherent statement of the rights of appeal in the English legal system, but the following principles seem to emerge as being of wide application.

1.3.13   First, there is usually one opportunity to appeal on the facts and the merits of the case, with the possibility of a series of appeals on the law.

1.3.14   Secondly, the initial opportunity of appeal will be available as a matter of right, but further appeal will be subject to obtaining leave to appeal, either from the court whose decision is being challenged or the court which will hear the appeal if it proceeds.

1.3.15   Thirdly, an acquittal by a jury — in other words, following a trial at the Crown Court — is such a fundamental safeguard of individual liberty that it will never be challengeable on appeal.

THE DOCTRINE OF BINDING PRECEDENT

1.4.01   Most people would probably accept that justice requires similar cases to be dealt with in a similar way. So there is nothing surprising in the fact that judges in developed legal systems tend to follow each other's decisions. What is unusual about the common law system is that, theoretically at least, in certain circumstances judges are *bound* to follow decisions made in earlier cases.

1.4.02   A system which guaranteed consistency between decisions in similar cases would meet another important requirement of any fair legal system, namely making it possible for lawyers to advise their clients with reasonable confidence as to the legal position. However, excessive rigidity would make it impossible for the courts to respond sympathetically to the particular subtleties of individual cases, and would also hamper the desirable development of the law.

1.4.03   One analysis of this problem presents the choice as being between certainty on the one hand and justice on the other. Such an analysis is, however, at best naive and at worst disingenuous, since sufficient certainty to enable reasonable predictability is itself a part of, rather than being opposed to, justice. It will be apparent, therefore, that it is a question of striking a broadly acceptable balance, rather than identifying a *right* answer.

1.4.04 An important aspect of the way in which the English legal system attempts to deal with this problem of reconciling the competing aims of predictability, flexibility and reform, is the doctrine of binding precedent. The doctrine, which is peculiar to the common law, is sometimes referred to by the Latin tag *stare decisis*, which may be roughly translated as '*to stand by decisions*'. A working statement of the doctrine could be:

> All courts bind all lower courts, and the Court of Appeal also binds itself, as does the House of Lords (although the position in both the Court of Appeal and the House of Lords is subject to detailed, and sometimes controversial, exceptions.

The outline diagram in 1.3.01 indicates the relative positions of the courts.

1.4.05 Strictly speaking, the European Court of Justice is not bound by its own decisions, but in practice it does tend to follow them.

1.4.06 Because the Judicial Committee of the Privy Council stands outside the hierarchy of the courts, strictly speaking its decisions are never binding on any other court, but remain of persuasive authority only. However, the fact that membership of the Judicial Committees of the House of Lords and the Privy Council are almost identical means that many Privy Council decisions are treated as being practically equivalent to House of Lords authorities. Naturally, as a consequence of judicial psychology, the Privy Council itself tends to follow its own decisions. although it is not bound to do so.

1.4.07 The doctrine of binding precedent does not apply to administrative tribunals, although these bodies do have a natural tendency to follow each other's decisions. Neither does the doctrine apply to statutory inquiries. In any event, inquiries are very heavily concerned with finding facts, so the idea of precedent would be of relatively little use.

1.4.08 Having dealt with the hierarchy of the courts, the idea of bindingness must be explored in a little more detail. Of course, the actual decision in any case in any court is always binding on the parties, subject only to the possibility of appeal to, or review by, a higher court. However, this is not what is meant by the doctrine of binding precedent. What the doctrine is concerned with is the provision of rules of law which will be capable of being applied by all later courts and will actually actually be binding on some of them.

1.4.09 The first point is that not every part of a judgment will be binding. To identify the binding part, a judgment must be analysed into two constituent elements: *ratio decidendi* and *obiter dicta*. The binding part is the ratio decidendi, which may be translated as '*the reason for the decision*'. The remainder of the judgment will be *obiter dicta*, which may be translated as '*sayings by the way*'.

1.4.10   The plural of *ratio decidendi* is either *ratios decidendi* or *rationes decidendi*, according to personal preference. The sentence in the previous paragraph which used the phrase *obiter dicta* required it to be given in its plural form: the singular is *obiter dictum*. It is conventional to speak of *ratio* and *dictum* − and their respective plurals − without using the other part of each phrase. The word *obiter* should never be used on its own as a noun, although it is acceptable as an adverb and an adjective.
1.4.11   One of the principal difficulties in reading cases centres on the need to identify the *ratio*. The difficulties involved in this process arise from the fact that a judge who is deciding a case is usually going to be principally concerned with the resolution of the issue between the parties. Therefore it is the circumstances of the instant case which will form the focus of his statement of the law. The fact that his decision will be subjected to detailed analysis in later cases will usually be of secondary importance to him. The point was well made by Lord Halsbury L.C. who said:

> the generality of the expressions which may be found . . . are not intended to be expositions of the whole law but govern and are qualified by the particular facts of the case (*Quinn v. Leathem* (1901)).

In other words, when looking for the *ratio* of a case, it will be necessary to identify the *material facts which influenced the formulation of the rule of law which was used to justify the decision.*
1.4.12   If the judge in a later case decides that the facts of an earlier case were materially different from the facts of the case before him, he can perfectly properly *distinguish* the earlier case. This is not a question of interfering with the authority of the earlier case in any subsequent cases which may be genuinely similar. It is simply a question of deciding that the earlier case is not relevant to the case which is currently being decided.
1.4.13   The importance of the technique of distinguishing cases must be stressed, since it is an important way in which judges seek to achieve results which they feel to be appropriate to the cases which they decide. No totally reliable formula for the identification of material facts exists, but an example may help to show how distinguishing can work in practice.
1.4.14   The case of *Burgess v. McCracken* (1986) arose from the commercial activities of a professional photographer in a public park. His method of business was to get people to agree to have their photographs taken. He then took their photographs and received a deposit. He subsequently sent them the photographs through the post, and they sent him the balance of his fee. It was important to know whether what he did in the park amounted to trading because if it did he was committing an offence. A magistrates' court acquitted him because an earlier case (*Newman v. Lipman* (1950)) had decided that exactly the same conduct

in a street did not amount to the offence of trading in the street.

1.4.15 However, in *Burgess* the prosecution successfully appealed to the High Court, where it was held that there was a legally relevant distinction between streets and parks. The court said that the offence in relation to streets was intended to prevent obstructions of the kind that can arise when traders set up stalls to display their goods. Street photographers do not do this, therefore they do not commit an offence. On the other hand, people go into parks for relaxation and recreation, therefore the offence in relation to parks has a wider purpose, which includes protecting people from annoyance. In this context, therefore the mere absence of obstruction did not justify an acquittal.

1.4.16 As a means of avoiding a consequence which he feels to be wrong, a judge may be tempted to distinguish an earlier case on artificial grounds. Indeed some people may feel that *Burgess* itself is an example of artificial distinguishing. However, leaving aside the merits of individual examples, the fact that artificial distinguishing does take place must be recognized. Similarly, it must be recognized that this undermines the predictability of the legal system. Nevertheless, the litigant who is disappointed as a result will have no recourse other than an appeal to a higher court.

1.4.17 The responsibility of the judges when considering whether to distinguish an earlier case is well explained by Robert Goff L.J.:

> In my opinion, although of course the courts of this country are bound by the doctrine of precedent, sensibly interpreted, nevertheless it would be irresponsible for judges to act as automata, rigidly applying authorities without regard to consequences. Where therefore it appears at first sight that authority compels a judge to reach a conclusion which he senses to be unjust or inappropriate, he is, I consider, under a positive duty to examine the relevant authorities with scrupulous care to ascertain whether he can, within the limits imposed by the doctrine of precedent (always sensibly interpreted), legitimately interpret or qualify the principle expressed in the authorities to achieve the result which he perceives to be just or appropriate in the particular case. I do not disguise the fact that I have sought to perform this function in the present case. (*Elliott v. C.* (1983)).

1.4.18 At first sight this attitude may seem to amount to a total denial of the doctrine of binding precedent. However, Robert Goff L.J. did indicate that there are 'limits imposed by the doctrine', and in the result, he actually felt unable to achieve the outcome which he perceived to be just or appropriate, saying he was 'constrained ... by authority' to reach a conclusion which caused him 'unhappiness'.

1.4.19 One of the classic textbooks on jurisprudence expresses the dynamism of the concept of *ratio* in literally graphic terms:

If we think of the rule of law as a line on a graph, then the case itself is like a point through which that line is drawn.' (*Salmond on Jurisprudence*, 12th edition, p.170).

1.4.20 Having established that the flexibility of precedent is, in practice, largely due to the technique of distinguishing previous cases so that they can then be disregarded, and to the possibility of interpreting and applying their *ratios* in such a way as to produce a just outcome, it is now necessary to turn to the concept of *dictum*.

1.4.21 Although as a matter of definition, *dicta* are not binding, it does not follow that they are entirely irrelevant. They can be said to have *persuasive* authority, meaning that a later court may choose to follow them, even though not obliged to do so. An important point here is that the degree of persuasiveness varies greatly. In fact the stage may be reached where there is little practical distinction between *ratio* and *dicta*. The explanation of this will be found in a consideration of the reasons why, in strict theory, *dicta* are not binding.

1.4.22 Two factors are relevant. One is that where a point is not central to the case, the advocates who appear will usually not argue the law, or if they do argue it, they will do so with less thoroughness than they would give to the main issues. Similarly, a judge who says something *obiter* will usually not have given the matter the same consideration as he would do if it were more central to the decision. It follows from this that if a point has actually been fully argued, and the court did actually give it very careful attention, there is no real reason why the court's views should not be treated as being authoritative. An example may be useful.

1.4.23 In *Hedley Byrne & Co. Ltd. v. Heller & Partners Ltd.* (1964), the facts were that the defendants had made an incorrect statement to the plaintiffs about the creditworthiness of a third party. The plaintiff relied on this statement and lost money as a result. The question was whether the defendants were liable to pay damages to the plaintiff. One complicating factor was that the defendants had expressly stated that they were giving the advice 'without responsibility'. In other words, they were making it clear that they would not consider themselves liable for any loss which resulted from their advice.

1.4.24 The House of Lords said that, in principle, the defendants ought to be liable. On the facts, however, the defendants had disclaimed liability, and therefore the plaintiffs failed to recover damages. If this is analysed into *ratio* and *dictum*, it will be apparent that the *ratio* was that the defendants had disclaimed liability. Since this was all that was necessary for the decision, all the rest of it must have been *obiter*. Nevertheless, the decision on the point of principle has been both generally accepted, and subsequently developed. The attitude of later courts faced with this kind of *dictum* may be found in the words of Cairns, J.:

> Where five members of the House of Lords have all said, after close examination of the authorities, that a certain type of tort exists, I think that a judge of first instance should proceed on the basis that it does exist, without pausing to embark on an investigation whether what was said was necessary to the ultimate decision. (*W. B. Anderson & Sons Ltd. v. Rhodes* (1967)).

1.4.25 The fact that *dicta* are of varying degrees of authority, from the almost worthless to the very strongly persuasive, leads to a sub-classification into *gratis dicta* at the lower end of the scale, and *judicial dicta* at the upper end.

1.4.26 Before leaving the topic of binding precedent, some reference must be made to equity. Although equity began as an exceptional and discretionary jurisdiction, during the seventeenth century its doctrines became systematized [paras. 1.2.07 *et seq.*]. Accordingly, there is now no doubt that, at the level of principle, equity is subject to the doctrine of binding precedent just as much as the common law is. It is at the level of applying principles to specific cases that equity still reveals its exceptional and discretionary origins [paras. 1.6.11 *et seq.*].

STATUTE LAW AND STATUTORY INTERPRETATION

1.5.01 Since the coming of the industrial revolution, social and economic changes have occurred at such a rate that the common law, whose development is dependent on the random process of suitable cases coming before the courts, has been unable to keep pace with the needs of the society it serves. As a result, statute law has become the major source of law.

1.5.02 It is a matter of fundamental English constitutional doctrine that Parliament is legislatively supreme. In other words, Parliament can enact any statute it wishes. There are major academic debates over the extent of the power (if any) of one Parliament to bind its successors, and over the relationship between European Community law and English law, but neither of these matters need be pursued for the present purposes.

1.5.03 What does need to be considered is the interpretation or construction of statutes. Judges use the terms *interpretation* and *construction* interchangeably on most occasions, and they can generally be taken to be synonymous.

Communication and interpretation

1.5.04 Essentially the drafting and interpretation of statutes is simply an exercise in communication. Having decided what it wants to do,

Parliament communicates the result to the world at large which is affected by it, and to the courts which have to enforce it. Before looking at how the system works, it is worth reflecting for a moment on the subtlety of communication in general. A great deal depends on the context in which a word is used.

1.5.05 If a shopkeeper displays a sign saying 'Pork Butcher' there is no doubt that he specializes in pig meat. If his sign says 'Family Butcher', nobody would think that he caters for cannibals. Yet both 'pork' and 'family' have the same grammatical function of qualifying 'butcher'. No problem of communication arises here because the shopkeeper and the public share a common code of understanding.

1.5.06 The processes of statutory drafting and interpretation create more than usually acute problems of communication because they involve a vital question of the balance of constitutional power. It is sometimes said that Parliament does not trust the courts, and that this leads to Parliament trying to envisage every possible eventuality, rather than laying down broad guidelines, and leaving the courts to exercise their own discretion. The detailed statutory provisions which result from this lack of trust inevitably cause problems of interpretation.

The traditional view of statutory interpretation

1.5.07 The traditional view of statutory interpretation is that the courts, being constitutionally subordinate to Parliament, should restrict themselves to identifying and applying the plain meaning of a statute (the *literal rule*).

1.5.08 However, even this traditional view acknowledges that there may be occasions when the literal rule may not produce a just solution, or indeed any solution at all. The result in a particular case may be absurd, or there may be an ambiguity as to the literal meaning. Under these circumstances, even traditionalists would allow the court to find an alternative meaning in the case of absurdity or to choose the more appropriate meaning where there is ambiguity (the *golden rule*). The third traditional perspective on statutory interpretation is that it is legitimate to have regard to the mischief at which the Act was aimed (the *mischief rule*).

1.5.09 These traditional perspectives may sound reasonable in the abstract, but they give rise to enormous difficulties in practice.

1.5.10 The first difficulty is that it may not be possible to identify the plain meaning of a word. In one case in the House of Lords, dealing with s. 1 of the Merchant Shipping (International Labour Conventions) Act 1925, Lord Tomlin said that the the relevant words were 'free from ambiguity', whereas Lord Blanesburgh said, 'I do not suggest that this Act . . . is clear' (*Ellerman Lines Ltd. v. Murray* (1930)).

1.5.11 Secondly, given the legislative supremacy of Parliament, how absurd must an outcome be to justify the courts in departing from the statutory language? For example, the case of *Whiteley v. Chappell* (1868) dealt with a statute under which it was an offence to impersonate 'any person entitled to vote' at an election. The defendant impersonated someone who had been entitled to vote, but who had died before the election took place. The court held that the defendant had not committed the offence, because dead men are not 'entitled to vote'. Most people would probably find little difficulty in calling this result 'absurd', yet the court did not do so. The flexibility which inevitably results from the highly subjective nature of the notion of absurdity obviously gives the courts very considerable power.

1.5.12 Thirdly, if the courts are to use the mischief rule, how are they to identify the mischief at which the Act was aimed, other than by having regard to the words of the Act itself? Are they, for example, to consult Hansard, the official report of proceedings in Parliament, to try to find out what the people who passed the Act thought it meant? If so, the lawyers who advise clients must do the same. But is it realistic to require a solicitor who is advising a client on, say, the Offences Against the Person Act 1861, to consult not only the Act itself and the cases decided under it, but also the relevant volumes of Hansard? Even if Hansard is used, will it help? Which of the many viewpoints expressed in debate can be identified as the one which represented Parliament's collective view of the mischief at which the Act was aimed? In fact there is a detailed body of case-law, which is by no means internally self-consistent, on the question of which extrinsic sources can be consulted and the conclusions which can be drawn from them.

Enlightened literalism and the purposive approach

1.5.13 The difficulties which result from the traditional approaches to statutory interpretation have led to an attitude which is perhaps best described as enlightened literalism or, more usually, the *purposive approach*. This approach emphasises the importance of identifying the context in which words occur before seeking their plain meaning, and it acknowledges that the purpose which underlies the statute is an important part of that context. The problem of identifying the purpose remains, but this does not seem to prevent the attainment of results which coincide with commonsense.

1.5.14 Not all judges are wholehearted purposivists, but the fact that purposivism is the dominant method of interpretation in European legal systems may give added impetus to its increasing acceptance in England. In any event, the approach is already sufficiently widely accepted for two examples of the way it works to be given.

1.5.15 First, in *Kammins Ballrooms Co. Ltd. v. Zenith Investments Ltd.* (1970), the House of Lords had to interpret the Landlord and Tenant Act 1954. Part of the scheme of the Act is that where a tenancy of business premises is about to expire, the tenant may request the grant of a new tenancy from his landlord. If the landlord opposes this request, the tenant then has the right to challenge him by applying to the county court, but s. 29(3) of the Act provides:

> no application . . . shall be entertained unless it is made not less than two nor more than four months after . . . the making of the tenant's request for a new tenancy.

In the present case the request was made before the minimum period of two months had elapsed. The point appears to have gone unnoticed for some time during the litigation, but eventually the landlords raised the matter and contended that, as a result, the court had no jurisdiction.

1.5.16 The House of Lords held that although the landlords' argument would succeed if the time limit was substantive, the argument would fail if the time limit was only procedural. Commenting on the statutory words, Lord Diplock said:

> semantics and the rules of syntax alone could never justify the conclusion that the words '*No* application . . . *shall be* entertained *unless* . . .' meant that some applications should be entertained notwithstanding that neither of the conditions which followed the word 'unless' was fulfilled.

1.5.17 However, his Lordship went on to say that the purposive approach could be used to achieve this result, because the underlying policy of the Act was to encourage landlords and tenants to agree between themselves. Furthermore, the time limit in question was clearly intended to benefit the landlords, who would be at risk of an application to the court for only a precisely fixed period. Therefore the court could promote the purpose of the Act by interpreting the time limit as being merely procedural, with the result that the landlords could agree to dispense with compliance if they so wished. The issue of fact therefore shifted from the simple question of when the application had been made, to the more complicated one of whether the landlords' conduct implied that they had waived compliance with the time limit.

1.5.18 Judges who rely on the purposive approach do not always use this phrase to indicate what they are doing, as can be seen from the case of *R. v. Pigg* (1983). The point at issue was whether the defendant's conviction for rape should be upheld or quashed. His conviction had been by a majority verdict. Section 17(2) of the Juries Act 1974 provides that:

a court shall not accept a majority verdict of guilty unless the foreman of the jury has stated in open court the number of jurors who respectively agreed to and dissented from the verdict.

What actually happened in *Pigg* was that the foreman merely said that ten jurors had agreed to convict the defendant, without stating that two had dissented.

1.5.19 Lord Brandon, with whom the other Law Lords all agreed, accepted that the statutory requirement had to be complied with, but he also said:

the precise form of words by which such compliance is achieved, so long as the effect is clear, is not material.

The conviction was, therefore, upheld. Lord Brandon appears not to have been concerned that his departure from literal interpretation resulted in the upholding of the conviction, although there is ample authority to the effect that the subject whose liberty is at stake, is entitled to the benefit of any doubt there may be as to the correct interpretation of a statute. Perhaps Lord Brandon's abhorrence of the offence weighed more heavily with him than did any traditional ideas of fair play for the defendant.

1.5.20 Although purposivism appears to give the judges considerable power its limits must be recognized. In particular, the purpose of any particular provision will be the same in all cases to which the provision is applied. Thus there is no real conflict between purposivism and the apparently uncompromising words of Lord Diplock, who, with the express agreement of the other Law Lords sitting with him, said that no court had discretion:

to vary the meaning of ... words ... to meet what ... the court happened to think was the justice of the particular case. Tempting though it might sound, to do so was the negation of the rule of law. (In *Re Energy Conversion Devices Inc.* (1982))

DAMAGES AND EQUITABLE REMEDIES

1.6.01 Where there has been an infringement of the civil law, the victim may well think of claiming damages. The basic principle of damages is that they:

should as nearly as possible ... put the party who has suffered in the same position as he would have been in if he had not sustained the wrong for which he is ... getting ... compensation (*Livingstone v. Rawyards Coal Co.* (1880)).

Quantifying damages – the compensation principle

1.6.02   The court may experience real difficulty in putting a financial value on the plaintiff's loss but, unless the extent of the loss is a matter of pure speculation, the court must do its best to quantify it.

1.6.03   In relatively routine cases, such as personal injuries, a basic scale of financial values for different degrees of injury to different parts of the body is constantly being developed and up-dated by the courts. In these cases the only significant variables are likely to be matters such as lost earning capacity. Other cases may be more challenging. In *Chaplin v. Hicks* (1911), the court put a financial value on the loss of an opportunity to take part in a beauty contest, even though the plaintiff may not have won anything anyway. The point was that the chance itself had a value.

Non-compensatory damages

1.6.04   In some cases the courts will deviate from the basic compensation principle and award a sum other than that which a genuine quantification of the loss requires. These are cases involving *contemptuous*, *nominal* and *punitive* – also known as *exemplary* – damages. Damages quantified according to the compensation principle are often known as *substantial* damages. All this means is that they are more than nominal, not that a large sum is necessarily involved.

1.6.05   An award of contemptuous damages is the court's way of showing that it regards the plaintiff with contempt for having brought the case, even though he has been technically successful. A typical case for contemptuous damages would be a libel action where the plaintiff has not actually suffered harm, and the bringing of the case has generated more publicity for the libel than it had originally had. Traditionally, they are the smallest coin of the realm, so currently they are one penny. The concept of contemptuous damages exists because, as will be remembered from the origins of equity, the common law has no discretion to refuse a remedy to a successful litigant.

1.6.06   Nominal damages are essentially different from contemptuous damages, even though they too are awarded where the plaintiff cannot prove actual loss. The difference is that by awarding nominal damages the court accepts that the plaintiff was right to bring his case. For example, in *Hanfstaengl. v. Smith & Son* (1905), the defendants had infringed the plaintiff's copyright. Even though he proved no loss, the plaintiff was awarded nominal damages to mark the fact that his rights had been infringed and to discourage others from undertaking more serious infringements in the future.

1.6.07   Traditionally, nominal damages are £2, although other small sums have been known. If there appears to be little difference between nominal and contemptuous damages the appearance is deceptive. The real significance of the distinction lies in the parties' liability in costs. The usual principle is that an unsuccessful party will be ordered to pay the legal costs of the successful party, and this will be applied in the case of nominal damages. In the event of contemptuous damages, however, there is a refinement to the usual practice. which results in the plaintiff paying the defendant's costs, even though the plaintiff has won. The plaintiff's victory, therefore is Pyrrhic, with one penny coming in and a far greater sum going out.

1.6.08 Punitive or exemplary damages are the third exception to the compensation principle. Here the court is deviating from the compensation principle by self-consciously awarding more than the plaintiff has lost, in order to punish the defendant and make an example of him. Punitive damages are available in three situations only (*Cassell & Co. Ltd. v. Broome* (1972)).

1.6.09 The first situation where punitive damages may be appropriate is where the defendant calculated to make more from his wrongdoing than the plaintiff would lose, and therefore more than the plaintiff could recover on a purely compensatory basis. The second situation is oppressive, arbitrary or unconstitutional action by servants of the government. In this context it is worth noticing that Lord Diplock made it clear in *Cassell* that the phrase 'servants of the government' should be widely interpreted, and should include, among others, local government employees. The third situation is where a statute authorizes punitive damages. This is extremely rare, and of no real practical significance.

1.6.10 Despite the exceptions, it is important to remember that the usual basis for damages is compensatory.

Equitable remedies

1.6.11 Cases where damages are difficult to quantify must be carefully distinguished from cases where damages are wholly inappropriate. In the latter type of case equity will recall its origins as an exceptional jurisdiction, created to fill the gaps left by the law, and will try to make a distinctively equitable contribution to the righting of wrongs. The entire range of equitable remedics cannot be covered here, but an indication of how they work can be given.

1.6.12 Specific performance is the order of the court which compels the defendant actually to perform his contract, rather than paying damages for failing to do so. For example, where there is a contract for the sale of a secondhand example of a popular model of a car, if the seller fails to perform the contract, the purchaser can easily buy a similar car elsewhere. The measure of the purchaser's damages will be the difference (if any) between the price originally agreed and the price actually paid. Because any loss will be capable of being compensated by money, damages will be an adequate remedy.

1.6.13 On the other hand, if there is a contract for the sale of an 'old master' painting, and the seller fails to perform the contract, no amount of money will enable the purchaser to acquire the practical equivalent of that painting elsewhere, simply because it has no practical equivalent. Therefore the court may compel the seller to perform his contract.

1.6.14 Similarly, if my neighbour erects a garden shed partly on my garden, he commits a trespass. If the court allows the shed to remain in position on payment of damages, effectively the court would be compelling me to sell my land to my neighbour. Since damages would be inadequate, the court could grant an injunction to restrain my neighbour from continuing the trespass.

1.6.15 The fact that equity began as a court of conscience, working justice where the law failed, has already been dealt with [paras. 1.2.07 *et seq.*]. This tradition still endures and, in particular, equity will look at the conduct of those who are seeking its aid. As one of the equitable maxims puts it, 'he who comes to equity must come with clean hands'. The operation of this principle can be illustrated by the case of *Gill v. Lewis* (1956).

1.6.16 The defendant was the tenant of a house. He fell behind with the rent, and the landlord obtained an order for possession. The tenant then found the money to pay the arrears. As the debt could now be paid, the tenant asked equity to prevent the landlord from enforcing the possession order. While in the house, however, the tenant had indecently assaulted two boys. As a result, the landlord argued that the tenant had not come with clean hands. The court rejected this argument because the indecent assaults were unconnected with the rent arrears.

1.6.17 In other words, the fact that the modern court which exercises equitable jurisdiction is the direct descendant of a court which came into being as a court of conscience does not entitle it to act as a general arbiter of morals, as opposed to the morality of the individuals concerned in the case in relation to each other.

ENGLISH LAW AND EUROPEAN COMMUNITY LAW

1.7.01 No modern treatment of the English legal system is complete without at least some mention of the European Community context. Strictly speaking there are three European Communities, namely the European Atomic Energy Commission (Euratom), which is concerned with nuclear energy policy, the European Coal and Steel Community (E.C.S.C.), whose remit is self-evident, and the European Economic Community (E.E.C.), which is probably the one which comes most readily to mind when the European Communities are mentioned. The only one which is relevant here is the E.E.C.

The English legal system and the legal structure of the E.E.C.

1.7.02   The E.E.C. was created by the Treaty of Rome in 1957, and the United Kingdom joined it at the beginning of 1973. From the point of view of the English legal system, the most important point is not that the United Kingdom became a signatory to the Treaty of Rome, but that Parliament passed the European Communities Act 1972, s. 2 of which incorporated E.E.C. law into English law. The significance of this is that, *as a matter of Community law, the laws of the individual member states must give way in the face of inconsistent provisions of Community law*. It is this proposition which gives rise to much of the anxiety about loss of sovereignty which many British politicians express, but in practice there have been relatively few examples of conflicts between Community law and English law, and it has usually not been too difficult to resolve those few conflicts which have arisen.

1.7.03   The four most important sources of E.E.C. law are the Treaty of Rome itself, rulings given by the European Court of Justice, and regulations and directives, which are both forms of Community legislation. 'Decisions' of the Commission or the Council of Ministers constitute another category of legislation, but these are principally used in the commercial field in contexts such as unfair trading practices, and therefore require no further comment here. Other categories of Community decision-making include 'opinions' and 'recommendations', but neither of these have any binding force, and so neither of them can be considered to be legislation in any strict sense of the term.

1.7.04   The Treaty of Rome is, for practical purposes, the equivalent of the constitution of the Community, and therefore it is obviously a source of law. Rulings given by the European Court of Justice, fall into two broad categories, namely the determination of disputes between member states, and the determination of points of Community law which arise in the course of litigation within member states. There is a special mechanism, created by Article 177 of the Treaty, under which a court of a member state can refer points to the European Court of Justice where a ruling on the community aspect of the case is necessary before the court of the member state can give its own judgment.

1.7.05   Regulations and directives may be made by either the Commission or the Council of Ministers. The Commission is the body which formulates the E.E.C's policies, and consists of one national from each member state. The Council of Ministers is a body of varying composition, which is also effectively the sovereign body of the E.E.C. The variability in its composition stems from the fact that the identity of the Ministers attending any of the Council's meetings will depend on the nature of the business to be discussed, so one day it may be all the Agriculture Ministers of the member states, whilst on another day it may be all the Finance Ministers, and so on. The distinction between regulations and directives is that regulations are always effective in themselves, whereas directives are usually effective only as to the result which is to be achieved. In other words, directives are instructions addressed to member states, directing them to achieve certain results within their own legal systems and within a specified timescale. However, the means by which those results are to be achieved will be left as a matter for the discretion of each government, depending on the constitutional mechanisms and practices of each member state.

1.7.06   The system of directives contains at least one major potential difficulty, namely that member states may be tempted not to implement a directive within the allotted time, with the intention of avoiding its effect altogether. To overcome this, the European Court of Justice has developed a doctrine under which, once the time for compliance has elapsed, the directive itself may be enforced against the member state which is in default, but not against individuals within that state, who are, of course, not responsible for their state's inaction. In this context, a broad interpretation is given to the expression 'member state', to include bodies such as local authorities and health authorities. The only limitation on this doctrine is that sometimes it cannot be applied, simply because the nature of directives results in some of them being worded in rather general terms, with the result that they are not sufficiently precise to be enforced by the courts.

1.7.07   One aspect of Community law and legal reasoning which many English lawyers find strange is that the traditional view of continental lawyers has always been that the process of statutory interpretation is principally concerned with identifying and promoting the intention of the legislature, rather than becoming involved in the kind of literalism that has often characterized the English approach. Naturally enough, from the outset the traditional continental approach was adopted by the European Court of Justice in relation to Community legislation. Admittedly, this so-called *purposive* or *teleological* technique of interpretation is now gaining ground in England [paras. 1.5.13 *et seq.*], but it still does not come naturally to many English lawyers.

1.7.08   Finally, it is worth noting that although from a British point of view it is conventional to think of any parliament as being a legislature, at the current stage in its evolution the European Parliament is not really a legislature at all, but is still principally a talking-shop (as the Norman-French *parler*, which is the origin of the word 'parliament', suggests that originally all such bodies were).

24

2 The legal context of the public library service

2.1.01   This chapter will begin by examining some fundamental elements of the British constitution, as a preliminary to a more extended discussion of two broad areas relating to the legal context within which librarians make many routine decisions. The first of these areas is the legal basis of the public library service; the second area is the law of contract.

CONSTITUTIONAL FUNDAMENTALS

2.2.01   Although the public library service is a familiar part of the domestic and municipal scene, its legal context cannot be properly understood without pursuing an excursion − albeit a short one − into the legal basis of the British constitution.

2.2.02   There are three basic British constitutional doctrines, namely the legislative supremacy of Parliament, the rule of law and the separation of powers.

2.2.03   Taking these in turn, the idea of the supremacy of Parliament was unequivocally established in the constitutional upheaval and re-settlement of 1688-89, when William and Mary agreed to accept the Crown on terms that they would rule by and with the consent of Parliament. This made any recurrence of the autocratic tendencies, which had then most recently been exhibited by the Stuarts, constitutionally impossible. For the present purposes we need not dwell upon the largely academic arguments about the significance of British membership of the EEC in relation to the supremacy of Parliament. However, it would be wholly artificial to ignore that in matters of politics the legal framework is only one factor which influences decisions and outcomes. In practice there are many political constraints, such as the political need to curry favour with the electorate and one's own back-benchers, which undoubtedly restrict the unbridled exercise of parliamentary supremacy.

2.2.04   The second doctrine is the rule of law. Although this phrase may be used in a general sense to indicate the idea that society is better when it is organised in accordance with rational rules which are created and administered by recognized institutions, in the present context it is used in a narrower and more technical sense. Briefly, the idea is that an essential element in preserving the freedom of the individual, and thus avoiding the imposition of State tyranny, is that the State, together with its organs and officials, should be subject to the due process of law in the courts, just as any private citizen would be.

2.2.05 The third doctrine is the separation of powers. The basic idea is that State activity can be divided into three categories — legislative, executive and judicial — and that the exercise of each category of power should be confined to the appropriate organs and officials of State. It is thought that in this way the freedom of the individual is best preserved, since although the government (the executive) may wish to introduce a new law, it cannot be enacted unless Parliament (the legislature) agrees that it is a good idea, and even then it will be up to the courts (the judiciary) to interpret and apply the law after it has been enacted. Despite its theoretical attractions, the separation of powers is by no means universally recognised in the British constitution. For example, the courts have a significant law-making power through the doctrine of binding precedent [paras. 1.4.01 *et seq*.]. Nevertheless, the doctrine does have significant utility if it serves to provide a warning of the potential danger which can arise when different categories of power are concentrated into one set of hands.

2.2.06 Some of the interaction of these doctrines can be illustrated by the case of *Burmah Oil Ltd. v. Lord Advocate* (1964). The House of Lords held that the British government was liable to compensate the owners of an oil refinery which was destroyed by British troops in the Second World War, who adopted a 'scorched earth' policy whilst retreating in the face of the Japanese. Parliament promptly passed the War Damage Act 1965, which retrospectively overruled the decision of the House of Lords, thus exempting the British taxpayer from any liability in the matter. In the end, therefore, Parliament won, as might be expected of a supreme body, but only after an independent judicial decision had been made.

2.2.07 This consideration of the constitutional background may seem rather far removed from the provision of the public library service, but in fact it has provided the necessary foundation upon which to build an understanding of local government law generally, which is, of course, the immediate legal context of the public library service.

THE LEGAL FRAMEWORK OF LOCAL GOVERNMENT

2.3.01 The framework of local government in England and Wales is largely a two tier affair, with functions being divided between county councils and district councils. (The fact that some district councils are called 'borough' councils, or 'city' councils is irrelevant to their legal status.) As far as most of England and Wales is concerned, the prsent framework was established by the Local Government Act 1972. As far as the London area was concerned, the London Government Act 1963 had established a system based on the Greater London Council and the London Borough Councils, and the 1972 Act applied this model to certain other heavily urbanized areas (Greater Manchester, Merseyside, Tyne & Wear, South Yorkshire, West Midlands, and West Yorkshire) which became known as Metropolitan Counties, each of which had its own county council, under which there was a second tier of Metropolitan District Councils. However, the Local Government Act 1985 abolished all the metropolitan county councils, including the Greater London Council, with the result that local government in those areas is now in the hands of the London (or Metropolitan) District (or Borough) Councils, together with certain statutory bodies which have taken over some of the upper tier roles, such as provision of police and fire services, previously performed by the Metropolitan County Councils.

2.3.02 The essential point about the legal framework of local government is that all local authorities are *legal persons*. This short statement has two major consequences, both of which must now be considered. Initially, however, it will be helpful to observe that there are two types of legal person: *corporations sole* and *corporations aggregate*.

2.3.03 Corporations sole are legal persons which have only one member at any given time. The classic example is the Crown. The fact that in practical governmental terms the Crown is represented by various Secretaries of State does not detract from the fact that there is only one monarch at any given time. On the other hand, corporations aggregate are legal persons with a number of members who enjoy membership simultaneously. The classic examples are companies (where the members are the shareholders), and local authorities (where the members are the councillors).

2.3.04 There is no necessary logic as to which organisations are legal persons and which are not. For example, in English law, companies are legal persons whereas partnerships are not: the inclusion of '& Co.' within the name of a partnership is no more than a convention and does not indicate that, as a matter of law, the organization has the status of a company. By way of contrast, in Scots Law partnerships are legal persons (s. 4(2), Partnership Act 1890).

2.3.05 The significance of legal personality is that whereas ordinary individuals (or in other words, natural persons) come and go through the natural processes of birth and death, all legal persons have *perpetual succession*, which means that the legal person continues in uninterrupted existence despite changes in membership. This means that the rights and obligations of the legal person are exactly that − rights and obligations of the legal person − rather than being the rights and obligations of the members individually. The practical importance of this cannot be overstated. For example, if a local authority enters into a legal obligation − for example a contract for the building of a new housing estate − the obligation will be the obligation of the authority and not of the individual members who voted for it. As a result of this, the authority will continue to be bound by the contract even though the membership of the authority changes, and notwithstanding the fact that the new members of the authority would not have voted for it. Similarly, the contracts of employment which exist between a local authority and its employees continue in unbroken existence despite changes in the membership of the authority − if the position were otherwise, a long-serving employee would be entering into a new contract of employment every few years as new councillors were elected.

2.3.06   The fact that a legal person is separate from its members can be illustrated by the classic company law case of *Salomon v. Salomon & Co. Ltd.* (1897). A leather merchant called Salomon, who had been trading on his own account, decided to form a company and then sell his business to the company. The company paid Salomon for the business in two ways − partly in cash and partly by giving him debentures. (Debentures are documents which acknowledge that a company owes money and − most importantly for the present purposes − give security for the loan. In other words a debenture is a sort of mortgage, so the borrower can enforce his right of repayment by going against the lender's property.) The company found itself in financial difficulties and various creditors were competing with each other to have their debts paid off first. One of the advantages of being a secured creditor − which Salomon was because of his debentures − is the gaining of priority over ordinary creditors whose loans are unsecured. Some of the ordinary creditors argued that it was unfair for Salomon to take priority over them because he was really the same person as the company. The court rejected this argument, on the basis that the company was a separate legal person and therefore Salomon's claim to priority payment was perfectly valid.

2.3.07   The fact of legal personality has another practical consequence, namely that the law takes a rather limited view of the powers of a legal person. More specifically, if a legal person tries to do something which in fact it has no power to do, the result will be legally ineffective because it will be *ultra vires* (or, in English beyond the powers of) the legal person concerned. Obviously this gives rise to the question of how the powers of a legal person are to be identified. In relation to natural persons, of course, the extent of an individual's powers, in terms of matters such as strength, intelligence and so on, are matters of fact. In the case of legal persons, however, since their existence is entirely a legal construct, it follows that the extent of their powers is also entirely a matter of law. Therefore in the case of legal persons, such as local authorities, which derive their existence from statute, the starting point for the identification of powers must be the relevant statute. In terms of the constitutional analysis with which this chapter began, therefore, Parliament decides what shall be the limits on the powers of each type of local authority, and thereafter it is the task of the courts to ensure that those limits are not breached.

2.3.08 There is seldom any difficulty in identifying the principal powers of each type of local authority. For example, in England the following are public library authorities: county councils, metropolitan district councils, London borough councils, the Common Council of the City of London. In Wales the corresponding authorites are county councils, along with any district councils designated for this purpose by the Secretary of State for Wales.

2.3.09 Moreover, local authorities have long been regarded as having power to do anything else which is reasonably incidental to those things which they are expressly authorized to do. This aspect of the law has now received statutory recognition in s. 111 of the Local Government Act 1972, but it may be best illustrated for the present purposes by the earlier case of *Attorney-General v. Smethwick Corporation* (1932). The corporation proposed to establish a printing, bookbinding and stationery works for purposes related to their statutory functions. This was held to be lawful provided that the activities were genuinely incidental to the corporation's other activities. In other words, to establish a unit to repair damaged library books will be reasonably incidental to the activities of a library authority, whereas establishing a free-standing book-binding business will not be.

2.3.10 Another useful statutory provision is to be found in s. 137 of the Local Government Act 1972, as amended by the Second Schedule to the Local Government and Housing Act 1989. Section 137 gives a local authority power to spend a limited amount of money each year on anything which, in their opinion, is in the interests of, and will bring direct benefit to, the whole or any part of their area, or to some or all of the inhabitants of their area. The limit on the amount of money which can be spent under s. 137 varies according to the type and population of the local authority involved. In each case the annual limit is calculated by multiplying a given amount of money by the 'relevant population of the authority's area'. According to the Act, the amount of money is £5.00 for metropolitan district councils and London borough councils, £3.50 for parish councils (and their Welsh counterparts, namely community councils), and £2.50 for county councils and non-metropolitan district councils. The method of calculating the 'relevant population of the authority's area' will be determined by the Secretary of State, who may also make Orders varying the sums of money specified in the Act. In all cases there are two important qualifications. First, s. 137 does not apply where the local authority have any other statutory authorization to spend money for the purpose in question. Secondly, the direct benefit which accrues must be commensurate with the amount of money to be spent. This version of s. 137 is necessitated by the introduction of the community charge (or poll tax), because the formula contained in the original version was based on the product of a 2p rate.

2.3.11 Specific statutory provisions, together with the *reasonably incidental* principle, will therefore suffice to indicate the scope of a local authority's powers. However, in a great many cases, those powers will require the exercise of discretion on the part of the local authority. Here again the doctrine of *ultra vires* becomes relevant, because the courts have developed a substantial body of law governing the principles according to which such discretion must be exercised.

2.3.12 It is worth pausing here for a moment to reflect on the constitutional analysis which opened this chapter. The separation of powers requires the courts to restrict themselves to judicial activities, and yet clearly if they start to control the way in which public bodies and their officials have exercised discretion, there is an ever-present danger that the courts will overstep the mark and start to substitute their own opinion of how the discretion ought to have been exercised. To deal with this difficulty, the courts repeatedly emphasize in such cases that their role is to assess the way in which a decision had been made, and not the actual content of the decision. For example, the case of *R. v. Devon County Council ex parte G* (1988) concerned a dispute between a parent and a local education authority over the (non-)availability of free school transport. In the Court of Appeal, Lord Donaldson M.R., in characteristically acerbic manner, said:

> Let me stress the role of the courts in this controversy. The school which the applicant attends, the parish council, Devon ratepayers and the media are all fully entitled to say that, if they were members of the education committee, the applicant would, of course, have been provided with free transport. And they have done so. Judges do not enjoy such a freedom. In ... proceedings such as these, their role is much more limited. They can only consider whether (a) the council misapplied the relevant law or (b) it reached a decision which no council properly applying the law could reasonably have reached.

2.3.13 Before turning to a detailed examination of how the courts actually control the exercise of discretion on the part of public decision-makers, it is important to notice, and reflect on, the fact that in terms of day-to-day administration, it is inevitable that public bodies of all sorts will delegate a great many of their functions, so that employees, committees, sub-committees and others may be performing functions on behalf of the public body. It follows from this that in these circumstances the person performing the delegated functions will, as a matter of law, be subject to the same constraints as the public body would be, otherwise delegation could simply be used as a means of avoiding those constraints.

2.3.14 In the context of local government, s. 101 of the Local Government Act 1972 specifically authorizes the delegation of functions to committees, sub-committees, employees, and even other local authorities. Lurking within this provision, however, is a problem which went unnoticed until the case of *R. v. Secretary of State for the Environment ex parte Hillingdon London Borough Council* (1986). The problem itself arises from the fact that it is commonplace for situations requiring emergency action to arise between committee meetings. The standard practice in these situations was for the committee's chairman to make whatever decision was necessary, and for the committee itself to ratify his decision in due course. However, in the *Hillingdon* case, the High Court, with which the Court of Appeal subsequently agreed, held that this practice was unlawful, and that decisions made on the basis of it were therefore void. The difficulty was that s. 101 authorizes delegation to *individuals* only if they are employees. If the delegation is to *members*, they must be constituted as a committee or sub-committee, and the courts held, as a matter of law, that there could not be a committee or a sub-committee with only one member, even if he was the chairman of the local authority or of the parent committee.

2.3.15 The *Hillingdon* case spawned two techniques which were designed to satisfy both the law and the needs of practical administration. First, there is the practice of delegating urgent matters to an employee, but subject to a condition that he must consult the chairman of the relevant committee before making a decision. Secondly, there is the practice of constituting Urgency Sub-Committees, capable of being convened very quickly, and therefore made up of members who are likely to be easily available at short notice. Neither of these solutions is ideal.

2.3.16 The problem with delegation to an employee, subject to consultation with the chairman, is that the exercise of discretion in the public sector must be made with regard to *all* material considerations [paras. 2.3.17 *et seq.*]. In practice, of course, it will be difficult for the employee to do anything other than simply implement the chairman's views. If the court took the view that this is what had happened in any particular case, the result would simply be that one kind of illegality would have been substituted for another. And yet if the employee does not implement the chairman's views, he may appear to be entering into the party-political arena himself. On the other hand, the problem with

31

Urgency Sub-Committees is that even they take *some* time to convene, while the practicalities of ill-health and the other hazards of life can also cause problems. Nevertheless, in politically contentious situations, Urgency Sub-Committees do seem, on balance, to be the better alternative, although probably the best possible outcome would be for some future court to decide that the *Hillingdon* case was wrongly decided, and that a committee or a sub-committee can lawfully consist of one person, and that that person can be the chairman of the local authority or of the parent committee.

2.3.17 Against this general background, it is now appropriate to consider what is probably the most famous single case in the whole field of judicial review, namely *Associated Provincial Picture Houses Ltd. v. Wednesbury Corporation* (1947). The facts were that the corporation, in exercise of their statutory power to license Sunday entertainments, granted a licence to the company, but imposed a condition that children under the age of 15 should not be admitted. When the company challenged the legality of this, the corporation argued that they could legitimately take the moral welfare of children into account. On the facts of the case, the Court of Appeal agreed with the corporation, but the real significance of the case lies in the following statement of general principle contained in the judgment of Lord Greene M.R. which is worth quoting *verbatim* and at some length, since it is the classic statement of the relevant law:

> When an executive discretion is entrusted by Parliament to a body such as the local authority in this case, what appears to be an exercise of that discretion can only be challenged in the courts in a strictly limited class of case. As I have said, it must always be remembered that *the court is not a court of appeal.* When discretion of this kind is granted, the law recognises certain principles upon which that discretion must be exercised, but within the four corners of those principles the discretion, in my opinion, is an absolute one, and cannot be questioned in any court of law. What then are those principles? They are well understood. They are principles which the court looks to in considering any question of discretion of this kind. *The exercise of such a discretion must be a real exercise of the discretion.* If, in the statute conferring the discretion, there is found to be, expressly or by implication, matters which the authority exercising the discretion ought to have regard to, then in exercising the discretion it must have regard to those matters. Conversely, if the nature of the subject matter and the general interpretation of the Act make it clear that certain matters would not be germane to the matter in question, the authority must disregard those irrelevant collateral matters. There may have been in the cases expressions used relating to the sort of things that authorities must not do ... I am not sure myself whether the

permissible grounds of attack cannot be defined under a single head. It has been perhaps a little bit confusing to find a series of grounds set out. *Bad faith, dishonesty — those, of course, stand by themselves — unreasonableness, attention given to extraneous circumstances, disregard of public policy and things like that have all been referred to*, according to the facts of individual cases, as being matters which are relevant to the question. *If they cannot all be confined under one head, they at any rate, I think, overlap to a very great extent.* For instance, we have heard in this case a great deal about the meaning of the word 'unreasonable'. It is true the discretion must be exercised reasonably. Now what does that mean? Lawyers familiar with the phraseology commonly used in relation to statutory discretions often use the word 'unreasonable' in a rather comprehensive sense. It has frequently been used, and is frequently used, as a general description of the things that must not be done. For instance, a person entrusted with a discretion must, so to speak, direct himself properly in law. He must call his own attention to the matters which he is bound to consider. He must exclude from his consideration matters which are irrelevant to what he has to consider. If he does not obey those rules, he may truly be said, and often is said, to be acting unreasonably. Similarly, *there may be something so absurd that no sensible person could ever dream that it lay within the powers of the authority.* [Emphasis added.]

2.3.18   In a nutshell, therefore, the *Wednesbury* principle relates to two aspects of the decision-making process: relevance and reasonableness. Before looking at these two matters in a little more detail, it is worth illustrating the distinction, and also noting some consequences in terms of the powers available to the court which grants an application based on *Wednesbury* grounds.

2.3.19   First, in the case of *Chertsey U.D.C. v. Mixnam's Properties*, (1964) the local authority, in exercising its powers under the Public Health Act 1936, issued a licence to the proprietor of a caravan site, subject to a number of conditions, relating to the terms on which the proprietor of the site could let the caravans to tenants. The court accepted that the council had acted in what it thought were the best interests of the tenants. Nevertheless the conditions were held to be unlawful because the statutory origins of the caravan site licensing provisions made it plain that the only relevant matters were those concerning the health and physical safety of the people living in the caravans, and not those concerning their welfare in a broader sense.

2.3.20   Secondly, the basic point that the court is concerned only with the decision-making process, and not with the content of the decision itself, can be expressed in another way. A challenge to the legality of the decision-making process is by way of *review* of that process, whereas a challenge to the content of the decision is an *appeal* against that decision. The crucial difference is that in an appeal the court is not only asking itself whether the decision was correct on its merits, but also usually has the power to substitute its own decision if it disagrees with the decision which is being challenged. In review cases, on the other hand, there is no power to substitute a decision, and, except to the extent that characterizing a decision as *unreasonable* amounts to an evaluation of that decision, the court is not concerned with whether or not it thinks that decison was correct. This, of course, gives rise to the question of what powers the court does possess in review cases. Broadly speaking, they fall into three categories.

2.3.21   First, the order known as *certiorari* (pronounced as 'sir-shore-rare-eye') is available to quash a decision. Secondly, the order known as *prohibition* is available to prohibit the pursuit of an illegal course of conduct. Thirdly, the order known as *mandamus* is available to compel someone to comply with the law. Other remedies which are also encountered include *declarations*, which are merely declaratory of what the law is, and have no enforcement mechanism associated with them, and *injunctions* [para. 1.6.14], which effectively serve the same purpose in the present context as *prohibition* and *mandamus*.

2.3.22   Three aspects of the procedure by way of application for judicial review need to be emphasized. First, there is no *right* to use this procedure: it is necessary at the initial stage to obtain the leave of the court to make the actual application. This requirement serves as a filter to eliminate petty, vindictive and generally unmeritorious applications. Secondly, the application is only available to someone with a particular interest in the matter which is being challenged: mere busybodies will not be allowed to make the challenge. Even if someone having a particular interest in a matter obtains leave to apply for judicial review, the case will still be brought in the name of the Crown. Thus if the court agrees to allow Mr Smith to bring a case against the Borsetshire County Council, the case will be known as *R. v. Borsetshire County Council ex parte Smith*. This means that the action is being nominally brought by the Crown on behalf of Mr Smith. In reality, the case will be conducted by Smith and his lawyers, with the lending of the Crown's name being a mere formality, reflecting to historical origins of the orders of prohibition, *mandamus* and *certiorari* as aspects of the royal prerogative.

2.3.23   Secondly, very short time limits have to be complied with in order to make an application for judicial review. There is some flexibility, but something in the region of three months from the date of the decision would be the usual maximum.

2.3.24   Thirdly, even if the applicant establishes his case, the remedies are discretionary. In other words, even if the applicant proves his case, the court may withhold the order which the applicant is seeking if, for example, the court feels that making the order would result in undue prejudice to the interests of good public administration.

2.3.25   Returning now to the heart of the *Wednesbury* principle, it will clearly be important to identify which considerations will be relevant in the context of any particular decision. Of course, it may be that the relevant statute deals with the matter explicitly, in which case there is unlikely to be any difficulty. In other cases, however, the courts must fall back on their own perceptions of the purpose of the statute, as in the *Chertsey* case.

2.3.26   There is very little case-law specifically relating to libraries in this context, apart from the case of *R. v. London Boroughs of Camden, Ealing and Hammersmith & Fulham ex parte Times Newspapers and Others* (1987). Section 7 of the Public Libraries and Museums Act 1964, which is more fully discussed at para. 2.4.03 *et seq.*, imposes on library authorities a duty:

> to provide a comprehensive and efficient library service . . . and for that purpose . . . to provide . . . such books and other materials . . . as may be requisite.

The facts of the case involved a number of councils who were all library authorities. The first applicants were newspaper and periodical proprietors, all of which were important examples of their type, while the other applicants were residents of the various councils' areas.

2.3.27   The newspaper proprietors were involved in an industrial dispute as a result of which they dismissed some of their employees. The local authorities gave support and encouragement to the employees by excluding some of the first applicants' publications from their public libraries. The sole reason for the ban in the case of two of the local authorities was the provision of a weapon in aid of the dismissed workers. The other local authority shared this reason for the ban, but also expressed the additional reason that some of the dismissed workers lived in their area.

2.3.28   The court held that the ban on the publications was inspired by the local authorities' political views, and the use of their powers under s. 7 of the 1964 Act for such purposes could not have been within the contemplation of Parliament, and that no rational local authority could have thought that such a ban could be legitimately imposed.

2.3.29   The decision in the *Times* case must be treated with caution. In particular, the law does not require political considerations to be left out of account altogether, provided *all relevant considerations* are put into the balance. For example, in *R. v. London Borough of Waltham Forest ex parte Waltham Forest Ratepayers' Action Group* (1988), the local authority resolved to make substantial increases in the rates. The applicants applied by way of judicial review, *inter alia*, to quash that decision. A major plank in the challenge was that some of the councillors who supported the increase had not made up their own minds, but had merely followed the party line. The Court of Appeal held that there was no illegality provided that the individual councillor remembers that whatever degree of importance he attaches to the unity of his political group and conformity with the policy of that group, the ultimate decision is for him alone as an individual, and unless he abdicates this personal responsibility, no question can arise as to the validity of his vote. More particularly, Stocker L.J. said that there is nothing morally or legally culpable in a councillor voting in support of a majority which has considered and rejected his arguments, provided that he considers all the available options and concludes that the maintenance of such unanimity is of greater value to the ratepayers than insistence on his own point of view.

2.3.30 Although the general proposition is that party-political factors are legally relevant considerations in local authority decision-making, some statutory exceptions have been made in relation to contracts made by local authorities. Section 17 of the Local Government Act 1988 is particularly relevant in this context, but full consideration will be deferred until paras. 2.7.02 *et seq.*

2.3.31 It is worth noticing that the courts have specifically acknowledged that changes in public opinion from time to time may legitimately be reflected in − and indeed may explain − changes of attitude on the part of democratically elected decision-makers. For example, in *R. v. Birmingham City Council ex parte Sheptonhurst Ltd.* (1988), the local authority refused to renew a sex shop licence which they had granted some years previously, even though there had been no change in the surrounding circumstances in the intervening period. The High Court refused to intervene in the local authority's decision, saying that Parliament must be taken to know that a local authority is a body of changing composition and shifting opinion, whose changes and shifts reflect the views of the local electorate.

2.3.32 One matter which the courts have repeatedly emphasized over the years is that there is what may loosely be called a fiduciary duty (i.e. the kind of duty which exists between a trustee and a beneficiary under the trust) in relation to the expenditure of public money. The point here is that although the money which is spent by local authorities will have come from a variety of sources, almost all of it has one essential characteristic: the people who contributed it had little or no choice in the matter. In fact this fiduciary duty has two branches. First, there is a duty to be fair as between different sections of the public. Secondly there is a duty to be fair to the public as a whole. The courts may not be entirely agreed as to the words which should be used to describe this duty, but the best way to indicate the idea may be to say that the relationship between the local authority and the public at large is rather like the relationship between a trustee and a beneficiary. The point may be illustrated by looking at a few cases.

2.3.33 In *Roberts v. Hopwood* (1925) the London Borough of Poplar had a council with a strongly socialist inclination. One example of how this worked in practice was that the council fixed the wages of its workers on the basis of how much the council thought they ought to earn. The wages which resulted were higher than average wages for comparable work. The district auditor intervened, and eventually the House of Lords had to decide whether the excessive wages were lawful. All the Law Lords agreed that the wages were not lawful, even though there was a statutory power to pay 'such . . . wages as . . . [the council] may think fit'. The reasons given for this conclusion varied, but Lord Atkinson remarked that the council had a duty 'to conduct the administration in a fairly businesslike manner with reasonable care, skill and caution'. Lord Sumner was a little more forthright when he said that the ratepayers were entitled to be protected 'from the effects on their pockets of honest stupidity or unpractical idealism'.

2.3.34 Another important case is *Prescott v. Birmingham Corporation* (1954) where the local authority started to give public transport concessions to old-age pensioners. The Court of Appeal held that although the corporation was not a trustee in any strict sense of the word, they nevertheless owed a duty which was similar to the duty which is imposed on a trustee. (In passing, it may be noted that the court's decision that the concessions were unlawful resulted in an Act of Parliament which specifically empowered local authorities to allow such concessions).

2.3.35 Perhaps the most authoritative statement in recent times emerged from the House of Lords in *Bromley London Borough Council v. Greater London Council* (1982). The Labour party campaigned in the elections for the Greater London Council on the basis that fares on London Transport should be substantially reduced, with the rates being increased in order to cover the loss. When Labour won the election and sought to implement this policy, the Conservative-controlled coucil of Bromley challenged its legality. The decision turned to a large extent on the interpretation of the Transport (London) Act 1969 but their Lordships also made certain comments of more general application. In particular, the point was made that one result of increasing the rates for the present purpose, was that central government grant would be lost as a direct result. So the House was not only dealing with a case of fairness as between one group (ratepayer) and another (public transport users), but also with a case where the total financial burden to be carried by the ratepayers was substantially increased. Since this increased burden would not lead to any corresponding improvement in services, the council was acting thriftlessly and unlawfully.

2.3.36 The immediately preceding paragraphs have centred on the *Wednesbury* principle of relevance, with only the *Times* case containing a passing mention of reasonableness. However, reasonableness is sufficiently important to merit some individual consideration. The key point is that the court is not asking itself whether it would have come to the same decision if it had had to determine the question: it is asking itself whether a reasonable decision-maker, having regard to the right considerations, could have made the decision. It follows that it will be extremely difficult to characterize a decision as unreasonable in this technical sense of the term. For example, in *Brinklow v. Secretary of State for the Environment* (1976) a local authority made a compulsory purchase order in respect of certain land, which they proposed to develop for housing. The site was a little unusual, with the result that the cost of the houses would be five times the going rate. The court acknowledged that the cost was high, but declined to say that it was so high that no reasonable local authority could have decided to incur it.

2.3.37 However, it must not be thought that the test of unreasonableness is entirely illusory. For example in *Backhouse v. Lambeth London Borough Council* (1972), local authorities were required by the Housing Finance Act 1972 to do one of two things: either they introduced a scheme of fair rents for their council houses, or they increased rents across the board by 50p per week. Lambeth did not want to do either, so they identified one council house which was vacant (and in such poor condition that it was unlikely ever to be let). They then increased its rent from £7 p.w. to £18,000 p.w., which meant that, averaged out across the whole of their housing stock, rents had been increased by 50 pence p.w. The court had no difficulty in holding this to be totally unreasonable.

2.3.38 The *Wednesbury* principle had been well-established for many years when Lord Diplock muddied the waters in the case of *Council of Civil Service Unions v. Minister for the Civil Service* (1984), which concerned the Prime Minister's decision to prohibit trade union membership on the part of employees at the Government Communication Headquarters at Cheltenham. This aspect of the facts, coupled with the length of the case's official name, explains why it is almost universally known as the *GCHQ* case. In the House of Lords, Lord Diplock said:

> one can conveniently classify under three heads the grounds upon which administrative action is subject to control by judicial review. The first ground I would call '*illegality*', the second '*irrationality*', and the third '*procedural impropriety*'. That is not to say that further development on a case by case basis may not in course of time add further grounds. I have in mind particularly the possible adoption of the principle of '*proportionality*' which is recognised in the administrative law of several of our fellow members of the European

Economic Community ... By '*illegality*' ... I mean that the decision-maker must understand correctly the law that regulates his decision-making power and must give effect to it ... By '*irrationality*' I mean what can now be succinctly referred to as '*Wednesbury unreasonableness*' ... I have described the third head as '*procedural impropriety*' rather than as failure to observe basic rules of natural justice or failure to act with procedural fairness towards the person who will be affected by the decision. [The topic of natural justice and procedural fairness is discussed in paras. 2.3.41 *et seq.*]. This is because susceptibility to judicial review under this head covers also failure by an administrative tribunal to observe procedural rules that are expressly laid down in the legislative instrument by which its jurisdiction is conferred, even though such failure does not involve any denial of natural justice. [Emphasis added.]

2.3.39   It is not at all clear what, if anything, is gained by reformulating the *Wednesbury* principle in this way. In fact, in the later case of *R. v. Devon County Council ex parte G.* (1988), in the Court of Appeal, Lord Donaldson M.R. said, of the term '*Wednesbury* unreasonable':

I eschew the synonym of 'irrational' because, although it is attractive as being shorter than '*Wednesbury unreasonable*' and has the imprimatur of Lord Diplock ... it is widely misunderstood by politicians, both local and national, and even more by their constituents, as casting doubt upon the mental capacity of the decision-maker, a matter which in practice is seldom if ever in issue.

2.3.40   All in all, therefore, the *GCHQ* case, although it must be mentioned as it is a modern decision of the highest authority, adds little, if anything, to this branch of the law.

2.3.41   Lord Diplock's reference, in the *GCHQ* case, to natural justice and procedural fairness is worth further comment, because failure to observe these principles is a very common ground for seeking judicial review.

2.3.42   It is probably beyond dispute that fairness should be one of the hallmarks of the decision-making process in the public sector. Indeed, in a sense the *Wednesbury* requirements of relevance and reasonableness are part and parcel of this larger whole, since decisions based on irrelevant matters or made unreasonably, can hardly be called fair. Nevertheless, the label of 'natural justice' is traditionally attached to a discrete body of law.

2.3.43   The traditional conception of natural justice is twofold. First a person has a right to be heard before a decision is made which will affect his rights, and secondly that the hearing should be conducted by a judge who is free from bias. A consideration of exactly what both these requirements mean is unnecessary here, because the modern view is that the strictest form of natural justice is relevant only in a judicial context, whilst a more relaxed approach can be taken in an administrative context. This statement does, of course, raise the question of what is meant by 'judicial' and 'administrative'.

2.3.44   In general terms, the distinction is that a judicial decision-making context is akin to that which occurs in a court, where there are two opposing parties and an independent judge, whilst an administrative context is less confrontational, with the competing interests being those of an individual on the one hand, and those of the public at large on the other. It follows that administrative decision-making is likely to involve an appreciation and application of policy considerations, although, of course, this must not be the the exclusion of all other relevant considerations [paras. 2.3.17 *et seq*.]. It will be apparent that this is the kind of process in which librarians are most likely to be involved.

2.3.45   The fact that the law requires administrative decisions to be made honestly must not be considered in isolation. The reality is that there is a very substantial overlap with the *Wednesbury* principle. For example, a librarian who, as a matter of policy, refuses to buy any books published by feminist publishing houses, may be said to be acting unfairly. He will also be failing to have regard to all relevant considerations, since he will not be balancing the interests of various sections of the public, nor will he be complying with s. 7 of the Public Libraries and Museums Act 1964 [para. 2.4.03]. Nevertheless, the law would not impose upon him the full rigours of judicial decision-making, so that, for example, he would be under no obligation to allow all the publishers' representatives in the country a hearing at which they could seek to persuade him to buy their wares.

2.3.46   It is now appropriate to examine the position of the public library service, and, for the sake of completeness, this will be followed by a comment on the position of the British Library.

THE POSITION OF THE PUBLIC LIBRARY SERVICE

2.4.01   The Public Libraries and Museums Act 1964, originally provided that local authorities' public library services should be under the supervision of the Secretary of State for Education and Science, with the assistance of two Library Advisory Councils, one each for England and Wales. Members of these Advisory Councils are appointed by the Secretary of State (s. 2 (1) and (2) of the 1964 Act). In practice, the Secretary of State's functions are now discharged by the Minister for the Arts, and the Advisory Councils have been superseded by the Library and Information Services Council.

2.4.02   Library authorities in England are the councils of shire counties and metropolitan districts, whilst in Wales they may be the councils of either counties or districts, although the approval of the Secretary of State must be obtained before a Welsh district can become a library authority (ss. 25 of the 1964 Act and ss. 206 and 207 of the Local Government Act 1972). Library authorities may, subject to the approval of the Secretary of State, provide library services on a joint basis. The machinery which enables this to happen is that the Secretary of State makes an order which creates a joint board (s. 5(1) of the 1964 Act).

2.4.03 It is the duty of every library authority to provide a comprehensive and efficient library service for anyone wishing to make use of it. This includes a *power* to lend books and other materials to anyone, but the *duty* to do so extends only for the benefit of people who live, work, or undergo full-time education in the authority's area (s. 7(1) of the 1964 Act). The distinction between the duty to lend and the power to lend is significant in relation to the ability to charge borrowers of certain types of items [para. 2.4.05].

2.4.04 The Act provides that, in fulfilling its duty, a library authority must have regard to three specific matters. The first matter is the maintenance of adequate stocks of books and other printed matter, as well as pictures, gramophone records, films and other materials, in sufficient number, range and quality to meet the needs of both adults and childrens, for the purposes of lending and reference. The second matter is encouraging people to use the library service. The third matter is co-operation with other relevant bodies, such, for example, as local education authorities (s. 7(2) of the 1964 Act)). The specification of these matters is, of course, without prejudice to the general requirement to have regard to *all* relevant considerations [para. 2.3.17 *et seq.*].

2.4.05 The provisions relating to charging for public library services are contained in s. 8 of the 1964 Act, as amended by s. 154 of the Local Government and Housing Act 1989. The amended version of the section provides that central government, acting through Ministerial regulations, can authorize library authorities to make charges for such library facilities as may be specified in the regulations. However, the section incorporates important exceptions, relating to both borrowing and reference facilities. First, the regulations cannot authorize charges in respect of lending written material to any person where there is a duty under s. 7(1) of the Act to make borrowing facilities available [see para. 2.4.03], provided that the material is readable without the use of electronic or other apparatus, and is lent on library premises (including buildings temporarily used for library purposes and vehicles used for mobile library purposes), and also provided that the borrower has not required any electronic or other apparatus to be used, or made available to him, for putting the material into readable form, in order that he may borrow it. On the reference side of library provision, regulations cannot authorize charges for reading written materials which are readable without the use of electronic or other apparatus, or which are in microform. Equally, the regulations cannot authorize charging for consulting catalogues, indexes and similar articles which are maintained exclusively for the purposes of the library authority's public library service, and this prohibition on charging applies irrespective of whether the consultation is done with the assistance of any person, or of any electronic or other apparatus. The amended form of s. 8 specifically preserves the practice of charging in respect of reservations and books which are returned damaged or late. (In passing, it may be worth commenting that the universal use of the word 'fine' to indicate a charge for an overdue book may be misleading, since in legal terminology the word 'fine' is used to indicate a financial penalty for breach of the criminal law.) The regulations can give discretion to library authorities in respect of the amount they charge, although the regulations may restrict any such discretion by specifying maximum charges. The regulations may also require library authorities to publicize their charges. There is a catch-all provision enabling the regulations to include matters which are incidental or supplemental to, or consequential on, the matters which are specifically authorized. Matters which are transitional, necessary or expedient, may also be covered. Finally, the regulations may make different provisions for different cases, including variations due to differences between people, circumstances and localities.

2.4.06   A local authority maintaining premises under the 1964 Act may itself use the premises, or allow someone else to use them with or without payment, for meetings, exhibitions and other events of an educational or cultural nature, and charges may be made for admission to such events (s. 20 of the 1964 Act).

2.4.07   If a complaint is made to the Secretary of State that any library authority has failed to perform its duties under the 1964 Act, the Secretary of State may cause an investigation to take place. If he is satisfied, after a local inquiry has been held, that there has been such a failure, the Secretary of State may apply to the High Court for an order of *mandamus* compelling the authority to perform its duties, or he may take certain administrative action instead. The possibilities are as follows. Where the defaulting authority is a Welsh district council, its status as a library authority may be ended. Where the defaulting authority is a joint board, it may be dissolved, and the library function transferred to its constituent local authorities. In any other case, the Secretary of State may himself assume responsibility for the library function in the area concerned, although in this case financial responsibility will remain with the defaulting authority (s. 10 of the 1964 Act).

The British Library

2.4.08   The British Library, which was created by the British Library Act 1972, originally consisted of the Reference Division, including the National Reference Library of Science and Invention; the Lending Division, including the National Lending Library for Science and Technology; the Bibliographic Services Division; the Central Administration; and the Research and Development Department. In 1985 the Reference and Lending Divisions were reorganized into two Service Areas, producing Humanities and Social Sciences, and Science, Technology and Industry; and the Science Reference and Information Service. The Library is under the control and management of a body known as the British Library Board, which consists of a chairman and not fewer than eight nor more than thirteen other members. The chairman is appointed by the Secretary of State for Education and Science, who also appoints all the other members, with the exception of one who is appointed by the Queen (s. 2 of the 1972 Act).

2.4.09   The broad purpose of the Library is to provide a national centre for reference, study and bibilographical and other information services, in relation both to scientific and technological matters and to the humanities (s. 1(2) of the 1972 Act). Among the Library's more specific functions is a power to lend items in connection with events of an educational, literary or cultural nature (s. 1 (4)). The Board makes an annual report to the Secretary of State, who then lays the report before Parliament (s. 4 (3) of the 1972 Act).

2.4.10   Generally speaking, the British Library is entitled to receive, free of charge, one copy of every book published within the United Kingdom, within one month of publication (s. 4(1) of the 1972 Act). There are, however, a number of exceptions to the generality of this principle, relating to works such as trade advertisements, calendars, public transport timetables, and other matters of local or ephemeral interest. Returning to the level of principle, a variety of statutes confer the right to receive copies, free of charge, on the Bodleian Library, Oxford; the University Library, Cambridge; the National Library of Scotland; the National Library of Wales; and the library of Trinity College, Dublin. In these cases, however, the right to receive material is dependent on the library in question making a written demand for the material it wishes to receive. The libraries which enjoy this right are the Bodleian Library, Oxford; the University Library, Cambridge; the National Library of Scotland; the National Library of Wales; and the library of Trinity College, Dublin.

COMPANIES UNDER THE CONTROL OR INFLUENCE OF LOCAL AUTHORITIES

2.5.01   Sections 68 *et seq.* of the Local Government and Housing Act 1989 make outline provision as to the way in which local authorities may exercise their powers to control or influence companies. This is most likely to be of concern to librarians in those areas where the inter-library loan system operates through regional bureaux which have been formed into companies.

2.5.02   A company is under local authority control if a majority of the company's shares are controlled by the authority. There is a sub-category of controlled companies known as companies which operate at arm's length from the authority. A company operates at arm's length if it enjoys a substantial degree of commercial independence from the authority.

2.5.03   A company is under local authority influence if it has a business relationship with the authority and either at least 20% of the total voting rights in the company are held by people associated with the authority, or at least 20% of the company's directors are associated with the authority.

2.5.04   The Secretary of State has power to make Orders 'regulating, forbidding or requiring the taking of certain actions or courses of action' (s. 70). Such Orders may differentiate between those controlled companies which operate at arm's length and those which do not, and also between controlled companies of both types on the one hand, and companies which are subject to local authorities' influence on the other.

THE LAW OF CONTRACT

2.6.01   There will be many occasions on which librarians will be involved in contractual situations, such as when ordering books or office equipment. The legal framework of the law of contract will, therefore, be considered here, although the question of the relationship between libraries and library users will be deferred until Chapter 7.

2.6.02   In simple terms, a contract can be said to be an agreement which the law will enforce. However, this statement does nothing to indicate which kinds of agreement fall within this category, and therefore it is only a description and not a definition. Fortunately, it is reasonably clear in most cases precisely what characteristics the law will require to be present before it will regard an agreement as being a contract. However, before considering those characteristics, it is essential to identify, and then to dispel, a very common misconception, namely that contracts must be in writing. The simple truth is that for virtually all contracts an oral agreement will be just as binding and enforceable as a written one. The major exceptions are contracts for the sale of land and consumer credit contracts where, in most cases, the law prescribes in some detail the kind of written evidence which will be required before the courts will enforce a contract. Additionally, of course, if a dispute arises as a result of which it is necessary to *prove* what was agreed, written evidence may be useful. Nevertheless, it is worth repeating the basic point, namely that in virtually all cases an oral agreement can constitute a fully binding and enforceable contract.

2.6.03 If an agreement is to be a contract, five elements must be present, namely offer, acceptance (both of which can conveniently be considered together), consideration, intention and capacity.

Offer and acceptance

2.6.04 The majority of contracts are formed when one party promises to do something and the other party promises to do something else in return. The mutual acceptance of the promises creates what is known as a bilateral contract. The most common and straightforward example of a bilateral contract is a contract for the sale of goods – which may relate to something as commonplace as a newspaper or a box of matches – where the mutual promises are, respectively, to hand over the money and to hand over the goods. In such examples, of course, no elaborate negotiations or formal statement of the parties' agreement is necessary, but this does not prevent the transaction from being a contract, and it is equally irrelevant that the entry into the contract and the performance of the contract are practically simultaneous.

2.6.05 Almost all contracts are of this bilateral nature, and the occasional and exceptional cases of unilateral contracts need not be discussed here.

2.6.06 An offer can, therefore, be described as an expression of willingness to enter into a contract on certain terms, the offer becomes binding once it has been accepted by the person to whom it is addressed. An offer may be oral, written or inferred from the offeror's conduct. The requirement that the terms must be certain is simply to ensure that both parties are aware of their obligations. It follows that the court will refuse to recognize an apparent agreement as being a contract if, on analysis, the terms are uncertain. Similarly, even where there is a contract, the court will refuse to enforce one or more of its terms in the event of uncertainty. This can be illustrated by the case of *Guthing v. Lynn* (1831), in which one party bought a horse from the other and promised to pay an additional sum if the horse proved to be 'lucky'. The court held that the term 'lucky' was too vague to be enforced, and therefore strictly speaking it could not have been part of the contract.

2.6.07 It can be important to distinguish between offers and other expressions of willingness to enter into contracts. For example, when a shopkeeper displays goods, or issues a catalogue, he would generally be regarded as offering to sell the goods. As a matter of legal analysis, however, what is happening is rather different: the shopkeeper is inviting the customer to make an ofer to buy, and there will be no contract until the shopkeeper accepts that offer. This may sound like a legal quibble but it can have important consequences. For example in *Pharmaceutical Society of Great Britain v. Boots Cash Chemists (Southern) Limited* (1953), the shop was organized on self-service lines, with goods being paid for at a cash desk in the usual way. Certain goods could only lawfully be sold under the supervision of a qualified pharmacist, and thus the question arose as to whether the goods were 'sold' − or in other words, whether the contract was made − when the customer picked them off the shelf, or when the money was tendered and accepted, at which stage a qualified pharmacist was in attendance. Holding the latter to be the correct legal analysis, Somervell L.J. drew an analogy with a bookshop where it is appropriate for the customer to browse before selecting a book to purchase, thus leading to the conclusion that it is the customer who makes the offer when he presents the goods at the cash desk and indicates that they are the ones which he wants. The shopkeeper accepts the offer by agreeing to sell.

2.6.08   The question of who is making the offer and who is accepting it may also be highly relevant in other circumstances. For example, it is obvious that revocation of an offer can only be effective if it occurs *before* the offer has been accepted, since any other rule would contradict the binding nature of contracts. Equally, the parties may agree that an offer will lapse if it is not accepted within a specified period, and even if there is no agreement to this effect the law will imply a term that the offer will lapse if it is not accepted within a reasonable period.

2.6.09   What is reasonable for these purposes will depend on all the facts of the case: if a rare book comes on the market, and excites a great deal of interest among collectors, the court might well say that it is reasonable for an offeror to know whether his offer has been accepted within quite a short period, whereas a customer buying a popular book by mail order could reasonably be expected to wait a few weeks before learning whether his offer has been accepted, by receiving either the book or a refund.

2.6.10   Finally, an offer will come to an end if it is rejected by the offeree, and in this context an attempt to accept an offer on different terms from those on which it was made will be regarded as a rejection. For example, in the case of *Hyde v. Wrench* (1840) the defendant offered to sell his farm for £1000. The plaintiff said that he would pay £950 for the farm, but, when the defendant declined to accept this, the plaintiff agreed to pay the original figure. The defendant then refused to proceed, arguing that his original offer of £1000 had been rejected and that it was therefore too late for the plaintiff to try to accept. The court agreed with this view, saying that the plaintiff had not accepted the offer, and that his attempt to vary the terms had amounted to the making of a 'counter-offer', which the defendant had then rejected.

2.6.11   An acceptance may be either written or oral and may even be inferred from conduct, provided in all cases that it is unqualified and does not purport to introduce any new terms, in which case it could be construed as a counter-offer or refusal. Lastly, it must be communicated to the offeror before the offer has been revoked. For example, an offeree who attempts to accept an offer by way of a crackly telephone line has not done so effectively unless the offeror hears the words of acceptance.

2.6.12   The main exception to the rule governing acceptance arises in relation to agreements which are concluded by post. The general rule (unless the parties have agreed otherwise) is that an offer communicated by post is only made when the offeree receives notification of the offer. This of course accords with the general principle relating to offers. In contrast, *acceptance* by post is complete and effective *as soon as the letter of acceptance is posted* (i.e. when it is under the control of the Post Office). The 'postal rule' applies only when it is reasonable to use the post as a means of communication and in practice the majority of commercial agreements specifically exclude its operation.

Consideration

2.6.13   Many legal systems regard an offer and an acceptance as being sufficient to create a contract, provided only that the parties intend to contract with each other. English law, however, is rather stricter, and requires an additional element, which it calls *consideration*. The essential point is that a contract is seen as resulting from the parties striking a bargain with each other, and therefore consideration is sometimes described as the 'price' which each party pays for the promise of the other. So, in the straightforward example of a sale of goods, the purchaser, by promising to pay the price, 'buys' the promise that he will receive the goods, and similarly the seller, by promising to transfer the goods, 'buys' the promise that he will receive payment. One consequence of this analysis is, of course, that a straightforward promise of a gift will not be enforceable because the potential donee will not have given any consideration for it. (Although it has little day-to-day significance, it perhaps just worth mentioning that the law does not require consideration where a contract takes the form of a deed. This is, however, the only exception to the requirement of consideration.)

The intention to enter into the contract

2.6.14   The proposition that English law does not consider an intention to enter into a contract to be sufficent to result in the creation of a contract must be handled carefully. Such an intention is not sufficent, but it is necessary. It follows from this, for example, that agreements which are social or domestic in origin are unlikely to be regarded as contracts. In many contexts, this principle will afford another reason, quite apart from the lack of consideration, why a straightforward promise of a gift will not be enforceable.

Capacity

2.6.15   The fifth element required for the creation of a binding contract is capacity. The general presumption is that any person is competent to enter into any contract which he wishes to make, provided that the contract is neither illegal, nor invalid for any other reason. Examples of illegality would include contracts whereby one party agrees to murder someone in return for payment by a third party, whilst other vitiating factors would include, for example, contracts between a prostitute and her clients, where the element of immorality will be sufficient to render the contract void, even though prostitution as such − as distinct from soliciting or running a brothel − is not illegal. There are, however, a number of exceptions to the presumption of contractual capacity, namely in the cases of legal persons, minors, drunkards and mental patients. Of these, only legal persons need be dealt with here.

2.6.16   The basic proposition is that a legal person can enter into any contract relating to any matter provided that that matter is within its powers [paras. 2.3.07 *et seq.*].

2.6.17   Obviously, at a practical level, a local authority can only operate through its human agents. This makes it necessary for a clearly defined scheme of delegation to be created, so that the powers of committees, sub-committees and individual employees are understood by all concerned. Each local authority, therefore, has its own Standing Orders governing this sort of thing, and these will include provisions relating to the making of contracts. Many routine matters, including the making of relatively small contracts, will usually be delegated to employees, and it will be under these provisions that librarians will most commonly enter into contracts for such matters as the purchase of books.

2.6.18   Since the provisions of Standing Orders will vary from one local authority to another, it may appear that outsiders dealing with local authorities will encounter practical difficulties in terms of knowing who is authorized to do what. In fact, s. 135(4) of the Local Government Act 1972 solves this problem by providing that a person who enters into a contract with a local authority shall not be bound to inquire whether the authority's Standing Orders have been observed, and that if there has been a breach of Standing Orders, the validity of the contract shall not be affected.

The effect of a contract

2.6.19 Although many terms of many contracts will be express — in other words, the parties will have specifically stated what the terms are — it is also very common to find terms which are implied. Obviously in relation to express terms, the main task for the courts is to interpret them and then to apply them to the facts, and there is little that can usefully be said about this process here. Equally obviously, in relation to implied terms there is a preliminary task for the courts, namely identifying which terms are to be implied into a given contract, because it is only after this has been done that the court can proceed to the interpretation and application of those terms.

2.6.20 There is a large body of law relating to implied terms, but for the present purposes it will be sufficient to identify and comment on certain provisions of the Sale of Goods Act 1979, which are derived from certain provisions of the Sale of Goods Act 1893.

2.6.21 First, where there is a sale by description, as would be the case, for example, where goods are selected from a catalogue, there is an implied term that the goods which will be delivered will correspond to the description of them which was given (s. 13 of the 1979 Act).

2.6.22 Secondly, where goods are sold in the course of a business, they must be of merchantable quality (s. 14(2)) of the 1979 Act). *Merchantable quality* means that the goods must be:

> as fit for the purpose or purposes for which goods of that kind are commonly bought as it is reasonable to expect, having regard to any description applied to them, the price, and all other relevant circumstances (*Bartlett v. Sidney Marcus Ltd.* (1965)).

2.6.23 Thirdly, where goods are sold in the course of a business, and the buyer, expressly or by implication, tells the seller the purpose for which he requires the goods, there will be an implied term that the goods will be reasonably fit for that purpose, unless the circumstances show that the buyer did not rely on the seller's skill or judgment, or that it would be unreasonable for him to do so (s. 14(3) of the 1979 Act).

2.6.24 Fourthly, where goods are sold by sample, as may well be the case, for example, when dealing with travelling sales representatives, there is an implied term that the goods delivered shall be free from defects rendering them unmerchantable, if those defects would not be apparent from a reasonable examination of the sample (s. 15(2) of the 1979 Act).

2.6.25 One difficulty raised by the Sale of Goods Act is that, in its nature and at the risk of stating the obvious, it applies only to sales of goods. This means that the principles contained in the Act could not be applied to certain other types of contract, such as office cleaning, which were clearly contracts for the supply of services, and not for the sale of goods. Similarly, although less clearly, the Sale of Goods Act probably has no relevance to certain hybrid transactions, usually known as contracts for work and materials, a commonplace example of which would be a contract with a glazier for the replacement of a broken window pane. The difficulty here is that although there is in one sense a sale of goods, namely the supply of the glass, it is inextricably intertwined with the provision of the skill and labour used in fitting it, and therefore it cannot be regarded as a straightforward sale of goods.

2.6.26 Some inroads were made into this difficulty with the enactment of the Supply of Goods and Services Act 1982. Read as a whole, the scope of the Act is wider than merely contracts for work and materials, but for the present purposes it is sufficient to note that in relation to the goods element of such contracts, ss. 3, 4(2), and 4(5) and (6), respectively imply terms which substantially correspond with those sections of the Sale of Goods Act 1979, dealing with sales by sample, merchantable quality, fitness for purpose and sales by sample. Finally, it should be noted that s. 13 of the 1982 Act provides that a person who supplies a service in the course of a business is impliedly undertaking to use reasonable care and skill in carrying out that service.

NEUTRALITY OF SELECTION

2.7.01 The application of the *Wednesbury* principle, and the overlap between this principle and the requirements of natural justice or fairness, have both been discussed already [paras. 2.3.17 *et seq.*]. It is apparent, therefore, that the principles of good librarianship in relation to neutrality of selection are entirely consistent with legal principle.

2.7.02 Additionally, however, Parliament has intervened, by means of s. 17 of the Local Government Act 1988, to prohibit local authorities from taking account of non-commercial factors when entering into contracts for the supply of goods, materials or services, or the execution of works. Although nobody would think that librarians were foremost in the legislative mind when this prohibition was enacted, they clearly fall within its scope.

2.7.03 'Non-commercial factors' are defined at some length in the Act, and include matters such as the rates of pay which a contractor pays his workforce, and the sexual and ethnic composition of that workforce; any involvement of a contractor in irrelevant fields of Government policy (for example, defence contracts); the involvement of a contractor in industrial disputes; the country of origin of supplies to, or the location in any country of, business interests of a contractor (South Africa being the obvious example here); the political, industrial or sectarian affiliations or interests of a contractor, or his directors, partners or employees, the key terms in this provision being defined in such a way that, for example, freemasonry is plainly included. Similarly, s. 18 of the Act, provides that, broadly speaking, the duty imposed by s. 71 of the Race Relations Act 1976 is also specifically excluded as a relevant factor. (Section 71 of the Race Relations Act 1976 requires local authorities to 'make appropriate arrangements with a view to securing that their various functions are carried out with due regard to the need (a) to eliminate unlawful racial discrimination; and (b) to promote equality of opportunity, and good relations, between persons of different racial groups'.)

2.7.04   Section 19(7) of the 1988 Act provides that enforcement of the provisions dealing with non-commercial considerations is by means of applications for judicial review and claims for damages by aggrieved contractors.

2.7.05   One other provision of the 1988 Act needs to be mentioned, namely s. 28. Part of the effect of this section is to prohibit local authorities from promoting homosexuality or publishing material with the intention of promoting homosexuality. The precise effect of this provision is not clear, particularly with regard to the meaning of *promote*, but until the courts have given any guidance, it would be an unduly timorous librarian who cleared all the works of authors such as Jean Genet from his shelves for fear of contravening the section.

2.7.06   Another factor which may affect the acquisition of material for libraries is the law relating to contempt of court. In essence, and very briefly, contempt of court can be said to consist of doing things which are likely to prejudice the administration of justice. Of course, a library authority's duty to provide a comprehensive library service [see s. 7 of the 1964 Act, discussed at paras. 2.4.03 *et seq.*] is important, but it is nevertheless only a very small part of the whole of English law, and the interpretation and application of the section may be influenced by other legal principles, including the law of contempt of court.

2.7.07   The leading case in the present context is *Attorney-General v. Observer Ltd. Re an Application by Derbyshire County Council* (1988). This case was only one of a long series of cases arising out the desire of Peter Wright, a former member of MI 5, to publish his memoirs, and the determination of the British government to do all that it lawfully could to prevent him from doing so. At one stage interlocutory injunctions were in force restraining various people from publishing the confidential information contained in Mr Wright's memoirs.

2.7.08   Derbyshire County Council, a library authority, against whom no injunctions were in force, wished not only to buy copies of Mr Wright's memoirs and make them available to the public, but also to stock newspapers and periodicals, without examining each of them to see whether it contained anything which would breach the interlocutory injunctions.

2.7.09   The High Court held that the local authority's duty to provide an efficient library service in accordance with s. 7 of the Public Libraries and Museums Act 1964, had to be read as being subject to a requirement that there should be no interference with the due administration of justice. In other words, the book could not be stocked. In respect of the other matter, however, the local authority fared somewhat better, with the court holding that the omission to examine publications to see whether they breached the terms of the injunctions could not constitute a contempt of court.

2.7.10 There is also the possibility of any local authority employee incurring criminal liability in relation to the circumstances surrounding a contract. Two areas of law are significant here. First, there is s. 117 of the Local Government Act 1972, and secondly there are the Public Bodies Corrupt Practices Acts of 1889 and 1916.

2.7.11 Under s. 117(1) of the 1972 Act, if it comes to the knowledge of any employee of a local authority that he has a pecuniary interest in any contract which has been or is proposed to be entered into by the local authority, the employee must give the local authority written notice of his interest. Failure to give this notice is an offence, punishable by a fine. It is important to emphasise that the interest must be pecuniary, but it must also be noted that it may be either direct or indirect. It is generally not difficult to identify *direct* interests − and for the avoidance of absurdity, the Act provides that a contract to which the employee is actually a party does not count for the present purposes, otherwise such things as an employee's own contract of employment would have to be notified to the employing authority − but there are detailed provisions relating to *indirect* interests.

2.7.12 Briefly, indirect interests include those which arise through being a shareholder in a company, or a member of a partnership, where the company or partnership is a party to the contract, and an employee is deemed to have an interest in an interest of his spouse, provided that they are living together and he knows of his spouse's interest. There is also a general exemption for interests which are so remote or insignificant that no reasonable person could consider it likely that the employee would be influenced by them. There is a further exemption in relation to interests which arise simply through the employee being an inhabitant of an area, a water consumer, or someone entitled to participate in a public service.

2.7.13 Section 117(2) of the 1972 Act makes it an offence, punishable by a fine, for any employee of a local authority to accept any fee or reward other than his proper remuneration.

2.7.14 The effect of the Acts of 1889 and 1916 is to make it an offence for public employees to seek or receive bribes, and to make it a corresponding offence for anyone else to offer or give bribes to public employees.

3 The law of defamation

3.1.01 The law of defamation covers two areas of the law of tort, namely libel and slander, which are largely, but by no means entirely, governed by the same principles. This chapter will explain the principles underlying both torts, and in doing so it will automatically highlight both the similarities and the differences between them. The related topic of criminal libel will be covered at the end of the chapter, as will the offence of blasphemous libel.

DEFAMATION GENERALLY

3.2.01 According to one of the leading judicial definitions, defamation is 'the publication of a false statement about someone, to his discredit' (*Scott v. Sampson* (1882)). The first point to notice is that *publication* is an essential element of liability in defamation. *Publication* is used here in a somewhat technical sense of *communication to a third party*. What exactly constitutes publication is a matter which will have to be considered in some detail below [paras. 3.4.02 *et seq.*] but the fact that publication is central to the concept of defamation is worth emphasizing at the very earliest stage, because it makes the point that the purpose of the tort of defamation is to protect interests in reputation. In other words, however abusive I may be to you when we are alone together, no question of defamation can arise provided that I restrict my abusive statements to those which relate exclusively to you. It is interesting to note that the position is somewhat different where *criminal* libel is concerned [para. 3.6.01 *et seq.*]

3.2.02 Recognition of the need for publication before there can be any question of tortious liability in defamation leads on to another basic point which highlights some of the difficulties which the law encounters when drawing the line between defamatory and non-defamatory statements. The problem, which a moment's thought makes obvious, is that any legal protection of one person's reputation must necessarily involve a corresponding restriction of everyone else's freedom of speech. Whilst an individual's interest in protecting his own reputation may be regarded as self-evident ('he that filches from me my good name, robs me of that which nought enriches him and makes me poor indeed'), it is also important to remember that protection of freedom of speech is generally considered to be one of the cornerstones of a liberal democracy, and therefore to be a matter of the highest public interest. It follows that in this area the law has to perform a delicate balancing act between public and private interests.

3.2.03 The distinctions which are illuminated by identifying the importance of publication as an element in the torts of defamation require rather more detailed consideration, as the immediately following paragraphs will show.

TYPES OF DEFAMATION

3.3.01   The proposition that defamation comprises both libel and slander raises two obvious questions: what is the difference between the two torts, and why does it matter whether a particular instance of defamation is classified as being libellous or slanderous?

The distinction between libel and slander

3.3.02   At a general level it is usually said that libel is the written word and slander is the spoken word. In many cases this simple distinction will prove to be adequate. However, both case-law and statute have clarified a number of cases which might appear to present problems according to this test. For example, defamatory statements in motion pictures are libels (*Youssoupoff v. Metro-Goldwyn-Mayer* (1934)), as are broadcasts on radio and television (s. 1, Defamation Act 1952), and statements made in the performance of a play (s. 4, Theatres Act 1968). The key to understanding these propositions lies in identifying the importance of the distinction between libel and slander, rather than in merely formulating the criteria for making the distinction.

3.3.03   Libel is actionable *per se*, whereas slander is usually actionable only on proof of special damage. In other words, the plaintiff in a libel action will succeed merely on proof of publication of the defamatory statement, whereas in slander the plaintiff must establish that he has actually suffered harm as a result of the publication of the defamatory statement. The reasoning behind this distinction throws light on why the three cases mentioned in the previous paragraph are classified as libels.

3.3.04   Generally speaking, where the spoken word is concerned, it will be possible to identify the hearers. Therefore if one of the hearers inflicts harm on the plaintiff as a result of what he has heard from the defendant,

54

it is not unreasonable to expect the plaintiff to be able to prove it. It follows that if he cannot prove that he has suffered harm, it is reasonable to assume that he has not actually done so.

3.3.05   Where the written word is concerned, however, it will normally be impossible to know precisely who has read the defamatory statement. Therefore the plaintiff cannot reasonably be expected to know what harm has been caused by the libel, because he can hardly prove how an unknown person who has read the libel would have acted if he had not read it.

3.3.06   To a large extent, therefore, the practical justification of the distinction between libel and slander appears to be based on the extent of the publication, rather than on its form, even though it will be obvious that the extent of publication does not provide a total explanation. For example, an oral statement made at a public meeting might well reach an audience which is both larger and less individually identifiable than that which would be reached by a volume of verse published privately in a limited edition. However, such exceptions do not detract from the validity of the general proposition, which remains useful as a means of explaining the special cases mentioned in para. 3.3.02.

3.3.07   The previous paragraphs have shown that in striking the balance between freedom of speech and protection of reputation, the law takes a stricter view of defamatory statements whose effects are more difficult to identify. However, this is not the only type of case which the law recognizes as being of exceptional seriousness. Certain types of slander are regarded as having sufficient potential for harming the plaintiff to justify him in succeeding, despite the normal rule that slander generally requires proof of special damage. The types of slander which fall into this category can be analysed under four sub-headings.

Allegations of certain types of crime

3.3.08   Where the defendant alleges that the plaintiff has committed a crime which is punishable by imprisonment, the slander will be actionable *per se*.

Imputation of certain types of disease

3.3.09   There is clear authority that an imputation that the plaintiff is suffering from a contagious venereal disease is a slander which is actionable *per se* (*Bloodworth v. Gray* (1844)). The reasoning behind making this type of slander into an exceptional case seems to depend on the fact that someone suffering from such a disease can be considered to constitute a hazard to other people's health, rather than that he is immoral, since a slander is not actionable *per se* where the imputation is merely that the plaintiff has suffered from such a disease in the past

(*Taylor v. Hall* (1742)). There is some slight authority to suggest that certain other diseases, such as leprosy, may be within the scope of the exception. Such authority as there is for this proposition is to be found in *Taylor v. Perkins* (1607), where the statement 'thou art a leprous knave' was held to be actionable *per se*, but such examples are probably of merely antiquarian interest, without practical significance in modern times.

Allegations relating to offices, professions, callings, trades or businesses

3.3.10   At common law a slander was actionable *per se* if it was spoken of the plaintiff in relation to his office, profession, calling, trade or business, and was calculated to disparage him in that context. The fact that both elements had to be present is clearly illustrated by the old case of *Jones v. Jones* (1916). An allegation that a school-teacher had committed adultery with a school cleaner was held not to be within the scope of the exception − in other words the plaintiff did have to establish special damage − because the court took the view that the statement did not refer to his competence as a teacher. Since s. 2 of the Defamation Act 1952, however, it is no longer necessary to establish that the words were spoken in relation to the office, etc., and therefore a case such as *Jones v. Jones* would be decided differently if it were to arise today.
3.3.11   In this context, the law draws a distinction between offices of profit and offices of honour. In the case of an office of profit, any allegation of incompetence was actionable *per se*, whereas in the case of an office of honour, an allegation of incompetence is actionable *per se* only if the allegation was such that it would justify removal from the office if it were true. A clear example of the distinction between the two types of situation is provided by local authority officers on the one hand, and councillors on the other.

Unchastity of a woman

3.3.12   The Slander of Women Act 1891 provides that 'words spoken and published . . . which impute unchastity or adultery to any woman or girl, shall not require special damage to render them actionable'. This provision appears to be self-explanatory, but it is worth commenting that the key concept of 'unchastity' has been held to include lesbianism (*Kerr v. Kennedy* (1942)).

THE ELEMENTS OF DEFAMATION

3.4.01   Having established that defamation is concerned with the protection of reputation, and having considered the basis for, and the significance of, the fundamental legal concepts involved, it is now appropriate to discuss each of the elements of defamation in more detail. The framework to be used is taken from the case of *Scott v. Sampson* (1882) [para. 3.2.01], namely that defamation consists of 'the publication of a false statement about someone, to his discredit'.

Publication

3.4.02 Basically, for the purposes of the law of defamation, 'publication' means no more than communication to a third party [para. 3.2.01].

3.4.03 Accidental publication – for example where the defendant makes a defamatory comment to the plaintiff personally and it is overheard by a third party – does not count, unless the defendant ought to have foreseen that he would be overheard (*Huth v. Huth* (1915)).

3.4.04 The qualification in terms of foreseeability explains the cases arising out of those situations where mail addressed to one person has in fact been opened and read by another person. In a domestic context it has been held that a husband can be expected to open a manila envelope, looking like a circular, even though it is addressed to his wife (*Theaker v. Richardson* (1962)), but not that a father can be expected to open a letter addressed to his son (*Powell v. Gelston* (1916)). In a business context, it has been held to be foreseeable that letters addressed to one person will be opened and read by subordinates – in other words, there is publication for which the defendant is liable – (*Pullman v. Hill* (1891)). Whether marking the envelope 'private' or 'personal' would be effective to negative liability is an open question. Presumably it would depend on the scale of the organization concerned, with a different view being taken of mail addressed to the chief executive of Marks and Spencer on the one hand, and mail addressed to the proprietor of a corner-shop on the other, with ample scope for argument in the middle ground between these extremes.

3.4.05 One other aspect of publication requires comment. Where one person publishes a statement, and another person who has power to terminate the publication chooses not to do so, that failure to terminate publication may itself be held to be publication. For example, in *Byrne v. Dean* (1937), a defamatory statement was published on the notice board of a golf club. The author of the statement was unknown, but the club's proprietors and secretary, who could have removed it but did not do so, were held to have published the statement. Clearly this principle would extend not only to notice boards but also to other equally well-known – if more informal and unsalubrious – media of communication, such as lavatory walls. However, the law is reluctant to put unreasonable burdens onto defendants, so if the defamatory statement is in permanent form, and its removal could be undertaken only at great inconvenience and expense, its non-removal will not amount to publication.

Falsity

3.4.06 Traditionally, the law has taken the view that in order to be defamatory a statement must be false. This can most conveniently be discussed in the context of defences to defamation [para. 3.5.04 *et seq.*].

Statement

3.4.07 With the exception of *Youssoupoff's* case [para. 3. 3.02], the cases considered so far have all dealt with statements in the form of words, either spoken or written, and obviously this will be the usual form of most defamatory statements. Nevertheless, it is clear that other means of communicating meaning can amount to defamatory statements. For example, in *Monson v. Tussauds* (1894), the defendant waxworks company placed an effigy of the plaintiff in the ante-chamber to the chamber of horrors. The plaintiff, who had been acquitted on a charge of murder, alleged that placing his effigy in such a position implied that the people represented were almost, if not quite, as evil as those whose effigies were in the chamber of horrors itself, and that in his case such a suggestion was inconsistent with his acquittal. The court held that he had been libelled. There is now some statutory clarification of the matter, with s. 16(1) of the Defamation Act 1952 providing that any reference in that Act to 'words'

> shall be construed as including a reference to pictures, visual images, gestures and other methods of signifying meaning.

The requirement of personal reference

3.4.08 Two points arise in relation to the requirement that a defamatory statement must be 'about someone'. First, does the reference to the plaintiff have to be intentional, and secondly is there any restriction on the kind of person who may be defamed?

3.4.09 It is clearly established that an intention to defame is *not* a prerequisite to liability. For example in *Hulton v. Jones* (1910), a newspaper published a fictional article to the effect that Englishmen abroad conduct themselves in ways which they would never contemplate whilst in England. As an example, the article referred to one Artemus Jones. A real-life Artemus Jones was held to be entitled to succeed in defamation. Similarly, in *Cassidy v. Daily* Mirror Newspapers Ltd. (1929), a photograph of Mr Cassidy, together with a woman, was accompanied by the caption 'Mr Cassidy, the racehorse owner and Miss X, whose engagement has been announced'. (The caption itself actually specified the name of Mr Cassidy's companion, but the judges were more coy and therefore the law report does not identify her.) Unknown to the newspaper's proprietors, Mr Cassidy was already married. The court held that his wife had been libelled, since a statement that her husband had just become engaged to Miss X could only be construed as meaning that he was not actually married to Mrs Cassidy at all, whereas it was widely known that she held herself out as being his wife. Another classic case involved a newspaper report of a bigamy trial, where the offender was identified as 'Harold Newstead, thirty year-old Camberwell man.' As originally written by the reporter, the story included details of the offender's address and occupation, but these were deleted in the sub-editing process. The court held that the report was defamatory of another Harold Newstead, who lived in Camberwell and was about the same age as the bigamist (*Newstead v. London Express Newspaper Ltd.* (1939)).

3.4.10 On the basis of the cases of *Hulton and Newstead*, it is clear that there is no legal effect in the conventional disclaimer, so beloved of novelists, that the incidents and characters portrayed in their books are purely imaginary and and that any similarity to actual events or real people is entirely co-incidental. At a purely practical level, of course, such a disclaimer may not be wholly otiose, since it may dissuade the uninformed reader, who feels he has been defamed, from pursuing the matter even to the point of taking legal advice. However, quite apart from such disclaimers, s. 4 of the Defamation Act 1952 may provide a defence in cases of innocent defamation [paras. 3.5.20 *et seq*.].

3.4.11 A particular problem about reference to the plaintiff arises in what are usually known as 'class libels', although the principles apply equally to 'class slanders'. This is the situation where the defamatory statement refers to all members of a particular group, and the question is whether an individual member of that group can sue on the basis that the statement is defamatory of him individually. The answer is that it depends on whether the statement can reasonably be understood as referring to each member of the class individually. The point can be illustrated by contrasting two cases.

3.4.12 In *Browne v. D.C. Thomson & Co. Ltd.* (1912) there had been publication of a statement to the effect that the Roman Catholic authorities in Queenstown had required the dismissal of all Protestant shop assistants. There were only seven people who exercised authority on behalf of the Roman Catholic church in Queenstown, and it was held that each of them individually could sue for libel. On the other hand, in *Knupffer v. London Express Newspaper Ltd.* (1944), an article was published in respect of a Russian political party which operated on an international basis with several thousand members, only twenty four of whom were in Britain. Furthermore, the article referred only to the party's activities in France and America. It was held that the leader of the party in Britain could not succeed in defamation.

3.4.13 The remaining question in relation to the requirement that the statement must be 'about someone' is whether there is any restriction on the kind of person who can be defamed. Basically, the answer is that there is no such restriction, but two points may usefully be made by way of clarification.

3.4.14 First, only a living plaintiff may sue. In other words a statement which attacks the reputation of the dead, however distasteful and unjustified the attack may be, cannot amount to defamation. Another aspect of this matter is that when a person dies, the usual principle is that his estate can pursue any legal claims which may have been vested in him at the time of his death. However, there is a small number of statutory exceptions to this principle, one of which is claims in defamation (s. Administration of Justice Act 1982). The second, and more positive point, is that actions in defamation are not restricted to natural persons. Legal persons, such as local authorities, also have reputations, in the defence of which they may invoke the law of defamation (*Bognor Regis Urban District Council v. Campion* (1972)). The concept of legal personality generally was explained in Chapter 2.

Discredit

3.4.15 Since the central concern of the law of defamation is the protection of the plaintiff's reputation, it follows that in order to be defamatory a statement must be to his discredit. The law has quite deliberately never defined this concept with any real precision, and all that can be done here is to consider the leading judicial pronouncements on the matter. In *Youssoupoff v. Metro-Goldwyn-Mayer* (1934) the court asked whether the effect of the statement would be to bring the plaintiff into 'hatred, ridicule or contempt, or cause him to be shunned or avoided', whilst in *Sim v. Stretch* (1936) the court asked 'would the words tend to lower the plaintiff in the estimation of right-thinking members of society generally?'.

3.4.16 Whichever standard test for defamation is actually adopted in any particular case, one thing is clear: it is the function of the judge to decide whether, as a matter of law, the statement is capable of being defamatory, and thereafter (provided that there is a jury which, unusually for a civil case, there almost always will be in a defamation trial), it is a matter for the jury to decide whether, as a matter of fact, the statement actually was defamatory. The allocation of this role to the jury makes it peculiarly difficult to predict the outcome of a defamation trial, but the conventional justification of the role of the jury is that it enables the decisions of the courts to keep abreast of changing public attitudes. For example, in *Youssoupoff's* case it was held to be defamatory to indicate that a princess of the Tsarist royal family had been raped by Rasputin. Whatever the attitude to such matters might have been when the case was heard in the 1930s, it is difficult to imagine that any modern jury would feel that simply being the subject of a violent and distressing crime would, in itself, involve any reflection on the victim's reputation. One aspect of the role of the jury which is much more difficult to justify is that they, rather than the judge, decide on the amount of damages to be awarded to a successful plaintiff. Lawyers generally feel that this leads to very much larger awards than would otherwise be the case, especially where show business and political personalities succeed against journalists.

DEFENCES TO ACTIONS IN DEFAMATION

3.5.01   It is in the context of defences to defamation that the law most noticeably performs its balancing act between the protection of reputation on the one hand and the protection of freedom of speech on the other. For example, in relation to a number of possible defences, although not in relation to all of them, the law will look more generously on a defendant who publishes a statement without malice, as compared with a defendant who publishes exactly the same statement in a malicious frame of mind. This differentiation is not altogether surprising, since it would be difficult to defend freedom of speech where that freedom is used maliciously to damage the plaintiff's reputation, but it does mean that before considering the topic of defences generally, it will be a useful preliminary to consider the meaning of 'malice' for the present purposes.

The meaning of *malice*

3.5.02   The starting point is that the defendant will be held to be malicious if he does not actually believe in the truth of his statement: 'If a man is proved to have stated that which he knew to be false, no one need inquire further' (*per* Brett L.J. in *Clark v. Molyneux* (1877)). However, if the defendant did believe in the truth of his statement, he may still be malicious. Thus in *Horrocks v. Lowe* (1974), the court held that 'malice' means 'spite or ill-will' and that 'gross prejudice and irrationality' are not enough, whilst over a century before that it had been established that 'any indirect motive other than a sense of duty is what the law calls malice' (*Dickson v. Wilton* (1859)).

3.5.03   Three miscellaneous points must be made in relation to malice. First, the burden is on the plaintiff to establish the existence of malice. Secondly, it is a matter for the jury to decide whether or not he has discharged this burden. Thirdly, irrespective of how the formulations cited in the previous paragraph may be interpreted in any particular case, it is clear that mere political opposition, or indeed animosity, will not

61

in itself constitute malice for the purposes of the law of defamation.

The defence of *justification*

3.5.04   The fact that the law of defamation is concerned with protecting reputations, explains the traditional view that a statement cannot be both defamatory and true, since this would amount to the law protecting a reputation to which the plaintiff was not actually entitled. Where the defendant relies on the truth of his statement, he is said to be pleading justification, because he is seeking to justify what he has said. The traditional view is that justification is a complete defence, so that if the defendant's statement is proved to be true, he will succeed even if he was motivated by malice, and even if he did not actually believe in the truth of his statement. By way of an aside, however, it is worth noticing that the Rehabilitation of Offenders Act 1974 has made some small inroad into the traditional view of justification as an absolute defence.

3.5.05   The idea underlying the Rehabilitation of Offenders Act 1974 is that most people should not be endlessly prejudiced as a result of convictions for relatively minor infringements of the criminal law. The means of achieving this is to introduce the closely related concepts of the 'rehabilitation period' and the 'spent conviction'. There is a great deal of detail contained in the Act, and regulations made under it, dealing in particular with exceptions in the case of people in certain types of employment, but the essential idea is quite straightforward.

3.5.06   Once a certain period of time ('the rehabilitation period') has elapsed following a conviction, the conviction becomes 'spent'. The significance of a conviction becoming 'spent' is that for most practical purposes the convicted person is entitled to treat himself, and be treated by others, as if he had never been convicted. For example, if an application form for a job asks whether the applicant has ever been convicted of a criminal offence, an applicant whose only convictions are 'spent' is entitled to answer the question in the negative, unless he falls within one of the exceptions to the scheme of the Act and the regulations made under it. The length of the rehabilitation period is determined by reference to a sliding scale depending on the severity of the sentence which was imposed. Convictions resulting in sentences of more than two and a half years imprisonment never become 'spent'.

3.5.07   It is worth noticing that the Rehabilitation of Offenders Act 1974 (Exceptions) Order 1975, includes among the exceptions:

> any ... employment concerned with the provision to persons aged under 18 of ... leisure and recreational facilities ... being ... employment of such a kind as to enable the holder to have access in the course of his normal duties to such persons, and any other office

or employment the normal duties of which are carried out wholly or partly on the premises where such provision takes place.

This appears to be sufficiently widely drafted to include at least some people, such as children's librarians, who are employed in the public library service.

3.5.08 The significance of the 1974 Act for the law of defamation is that if the defendant publishes the fact that the plaintiff has a spent conviction, the truth of the statement will not constitute a defence if the defendant was motivated by malice (s. 8 of the Act). It is, however, of the first importance, in terms of general principle, to remember that this provision is wholly exceptional, and that in all other cases truth is an absolute defence to an action in defamation.

3.5.09 In order to succeed in a plea of justification, the defendant does not have to prove that every element of his statement is true, provided he can prove that it is substantially true. For example, a statement that the plaintiff had been sentenced to a fine, with an alternative of three weeks' imprisonment was justified even though the alternative was actually only two weeks' imprisonment (*Alexander v. North Eastern Railway Co.* (1865)). However, at common law this principle did not apply to the situation where a statement contained a number of distinct allegations. Here the position was that unless the defendant could prove the truth of each allegation, the whole defence failed. The harshness of this rule has been mitigated by s. 5 of the Defamation Act 1952, which is to the effect that justification will succeed even if all the allegations are not justified, provided that, in the light of the allegations which are justified, the remaining allegations do not materially harm the plaintiff's reputation. The effect of s. 5, therefore, is to apply the principle in *Alexander's* case to a situation where there are several distinct allegations.

Absolute privilege

3.5.10 The law takes the view that there are certain contexts in which the public interest in the preservation of freedom of speech overrides absolutely all other interests: these are said to be occasions giving rise to a defence of absolute privilege. The absolute quality of the privilege means that the defendant will succeed even if he was motivated by malice, and even if he knew that his statement was untrue. Obviously the law will keep a very tight rein on the number of situations which can give rise to this type of privilege, and only five such situations exist.

3.5.11 The five situations giving rise to absolute privilege are (a) statements in Parliament; (b) communications between high-ranking officers of state; (c) statements made in court proceedings; (d) fair and accurate reports of court proceedings, provided they are published contemporaneously with those proceedings; and (e) communications between a solicitor and his client. The reasons for according absolute privilege to each of these situations are more or less self-evident, but in relation to the last one it is worth pointing out that, in the context of local government, the solicitor to a local authority is in a solicitor/client relationship with the local authority itself, in its capacity as a legal person. It follows that his communications with his fellow officers − except for those exercising delegated functions on behalf of the local authority, who would effectively be the equivalent of the local authority − and even with individual councillors, will not normally fall within the scope of this defence. Admittedly, other defences, such as qualified privilege and fair comment on a matter of public interest [paras. 3.5.12 *et seq.*], as well as justification [paras. 3.5.04 *et seq.*], may be available to a solicitor under these circumstances, depending on all the facts of the case. However, none of these other defences is as favourable as absolute privilege, where all the defendant has to establish is that he falls within one of the recognized categories.

Qualified privilege

3.5.12   As the term itself suggests, the defence of *qualified* privilege is significantly weaker than the defence of *absolute* privilege, although it shares with that defence the essential characteristic of operating in respect of untrue statements. The essential *qualification* contained in the title of the defence, is that it will be defeated by malice [para. 3.5.02]. In practice, an additional limitation is that the situations in which this version of the defence will be available are less clearly defined. The classic statement is to be found in *Adam v. Ward* (1917), where the House of Lords said that qualified privilege could arise only:

> where the person who makes a communication has an interest or a duty (legal, social, or moral) to make it, and the person to whom it is made has a corresponding interest or duty to receive it.

3.5.13   The requirement of a shared interest or duty may be illustrated by an example of a school-teacher who suspects that a particular child has been stealing. If the school-teacher tells the child's parent, the defence of qualified privilege will be available, because both the school-teacher and the parent have a shared interest in the development of the child's moral character. On the other hand, if the school-teacher tells someone completely unconnected with the child, the essential reciprocity of interest will be lacking, and therefore the defence will not be available.

3.5.14   It follows that the defence of qualified privilege can be defeated by publication which is too wide. A leading example is the case of *De Buse v. McCarthy* (1942), where the Town Clerk of Stepney issued a notice convening a meeting of the council. The agenda papers accompanying the notice included a preliminary report of a committee concerning the loss of petrol from one of the council's depots. In accordance with long-established practice, copies of the notice and all the associated papers were sent to public libraries in the area. The court held that the extent of the publication of the report destroyed the privilege which would have attached to it if it had been circulated only to the council members. In other words, the general body of rate-payers did not have a sufficient interest in what was, at that stage, only a preliminary report. In this type of situation there is sometimes said to be 'an excess of privilege', but it must be noted that the word 'excess' is being used to indicate that the boundaries of the privilege have been exceeded, rather than that there is too much of the privilege.

3.5.15 There is no closed category of cases to which the defence of qualified privilege will be available. In each case where the matter is raised the task for the court will basically be to apply the test propounded in *Adam v. Ward*. However, for the sake of completeness, it may be noted that s. 7 of the Defamation Act 1952 specifically applies the defence to reports of certain types of proceedings, e.g. disciplinary proceedings of professional bodies, meetings of local authorities, and meetings held for the furtherance of discussion of any matter of public concern, provided that the purpose of the meeting is lawful, but irrespective of whether admission to the meeting is general or restricted.

Fair comment on a matter of public interest

3.5.16 We have already noted that the defence of justification operates to protect the defendant where the defamatory statement is factual and the facts are true. Where the essence of the defamatory statement is contained in a statement of comment or opinion, it follows that justification will not be appropriate, because such statements do not, by definition, purport to communicate factual information. It is here that the defence of fair comment on a matter of public interest comes into play. At the outset it must be emphasized that a vital element of the defence of fair comment is, as the phrase itself indicates, that the comment must be fair. In other words, a defendant motivated by malice will not succeed in establishing this defence.

3.5.17 The classic statement of the requirement of fairness in this context is contained in the following words of Lord Denning M.R. in the Court of Appeal in *Slim v. The Daily Telegraph* (1968):

If he was an honest man expressing his genuine opinion on a subject of public interest, then no matter that his words conveyed derogatory imputations: no matter that his opinion was wrong or exaggerated or prejudiced; and no matter that it was badly expressed so that other people read all sorts of innuendoes into it; nevertheless, he has a good defence of fair comment.

3.5.18   As the title of the defence itself indicates, an essential element is that the comment must be on a matter of public interest. Clearly this means a matter of *legitimate* public interest, in the sense of public concern, and not merely matters of, for example, lascivious or scandalous interest. In this connection it should be noted that the private life of a person who holds a public position, will be a matter of public interest for the present purposes if, and only if, the private conduct relates to some quality, such as integrity, which is required by the public office (*Seymour v. Butterworth* (1862)). However, as a general proposition, anything which is put before the public for its appraisal becomes a matter of public interest for these purposes, so that, for example, a book reviewer may claim the protection of the defence (*Thomas v. Bradbury, Agnew & Co. Ltd.* (1906)). Perhaps more obviously, within the scope of the defence are matters of public administration (*Henwood v. Harrison* (1872)), including local government (*Purcell v. Sowler* (1887)).

3.5.19   Although the essence of the defence is concerned with the fairness of comment and opinion, it is nevertheless also central to the defence that the comment or opinion should be based on statements of fact which are true. At common law the position was that the defendant had to prove the truth of *all* the facts on which his comment or opinion was based. Under s. 6 of the Defamation Act 1952, however, it is sufficient if *some* of the facts are proved to be true, provided that the comment or opinion remains fair in the light of those facts. For example, suppose the plaintiff is a school-teacher and the defendant says of him, 'He is not fit to be a school-teacher. He has ten convictions for indecent assault on children.' The defence of fair comment would (after the 1952 Act) succeed even if the defendant were able to prove only that the plaintiff had eight such convictions, because the comment would still be fair even against this factual background. However, even after the 1952 Act, the defence will fail if the only contravention of the criminal law which the defendant can show is that the plaintiff has been convicted of, say, speeding.

Defences relating to innocent defamation generally

3.5.20   Although basically it is no defence for the defendant to say 'But I never intended to harm the plaintiff's reputation, therefore I should not be held liable', the law's concern with protecting freedom of speech is so great that there are a number of situations in which a defendant whose defamation is innocent may find he has a defence. The defence of innocent defamation is best considered under three headings, namely mechanical distributors, the defence of apology under s. 2 of the Libel

Act 1843, and offers of amends under s. 4 of the Defamation Act 1952.

Innocent defamation by mechanical distributors

3.5.21 Anyone who communicates a statement to a third party can be said to have published the statement [para. 3.4.02]. Clearly this covers a large range of people, such as booksellers, newsvendors and librarians, who merely distribute material in a mechanical manner, and on whom it would usually be wholly unfair to impose responsibility for the contents of the material. In relation to such distributors, Romer L.J. once said in the Court of Appeal, that there would be a defence for:

> a person who is not the printer or the first or main publisher of a work which contains a libel, but has only taken what I may call a subordinate part in disseminating it, . . . if he succeeds in showing (1) that he was innocent of any knowledge of the libel contained in the work disseminated by him, (2) that there was nothing in the work or the circumstances under which it came to him or was disseminated by him which ought to have led him to suppoose that it contained a libel, and (3) that, when the work was disseminated by him, it was not by any negligence on his part that he did not know that it contained a libel (*Vizetelly v. Mudie's Select Library Ltd.* (1900)).

3.5.22 Whether any specific mechanical distributor can bring himself within the criteria specified by Romer L.J. will, of course, depend on the circumstances of each case. In *Vizetelly* itself, the defence failed because the library company had ignored a circular issued by the publishers of the book, requesting the return of copies so that they could remove a page containing a defamatory statement. Furthermore, the library company did not employ anyone to read the novels in their library with a view to looking for libels. In the later case of *Weldon v. Times Book Co. Ltd.* (1911), Lord Romer M.R. (as he had become since *Vizetelly*) returned to the same topic, saying that there may be a duty on mechanical distributors to scrutinize some books carefully, because of their titles, or because of the recognized propensity of their authors to publish libels, but this did not mean that there was a general obligation to read every book which is distributed, in order to ascertain whether or not it is libellous.

Innocent defamation and apology under the Libel Act 1843

3.5.23 Section 2 of the Libel Act 1843 provides that where there is an action for a libel contained in any public newspaper or other periodical publication, the defendant will succeed if he shows that the libel was published without actual malice or gross negligence, and that before the start of the action for libel, or as soon as possible thereafter, he published a full apology and paid money into court by way of amends. This defence is very seldom used in practice.

Innocent defamation and offer of amends under the Defamation Act 1952

3.5.24   A defendant will succeed under s. 4 of the Defamation Act 1952 if he can show that the publication of the defamatory statement was innocent, and that the plaintiff has refused to accept his offer to publish a correction and apology as soon as practicable. In order to establish that the defamation was innocent for these purposes, the defendant must show two things. First, that he exercised all reasonable care in relation to the publication. Secondly, either that he did not intend to publish the defamatory statement in relation to the plaintiff and that he did not know of circumstances by reason of which the statement might be understood to refer to the plaintiff, or alternatively that the statement was not self-evidently defamatory and that the defendant did not know of circumstances by reason of which the statement might be understood to be defamatory of the plaintiff. The first of the alternatives making up the second part of the test would be useful to the defendant if a case such as *Hulton v. Jones* (1910) were to come before the court today, and the second could similarly be useful in circumstances such as those which arose in *Cassidy v. Daily Mirror Newspapers Ltd.* (1929) [para. 3.4.09]. It may be noted that s. 4 does not require the payment of any money into court. The only other point to note in relation to s. 4 is that a defendant who is not the author of the defamatory statement must show that the author acted without malice. In purely practical terms, of course, the task of proving either a negative situation or the state of some other person's mind, will usually be extremely difficult: to have to prove both at the same time will often be impossible.

CRIMINAL LIBEL

3.6.01   Having considered at some length the tortious aspects of defamation, it is now necessary to turn to the criminal aspects of the subject. The first point of importance is that only libel and not slander can be a crime. The second point is that there have been very few prosecutions for criminal libel in modern times, which means that the courts have had correspondingly few opportunities to clarify many of the finer points of the offence. Nevertheless, a brief account of the main elements of the offence can be given.

3.6.02   The first point to note is that there are two distinct offences of criminal libel, one arising at common law, whilst the other was created by statute, although even in respect of the common law offence, the maximum sentence is limited by statute to one year's imprisonment

(s. 5, Libel Act 1843).

3.6.03   Taking the common law offence first, Viscount Dilhorne made it plain in *R. v. Wells Street Magistrates' Court ex parte Deakin* (1979) that the test for defamation is whether the statement in question would bring the plaintiff into hatred, ridicule and contempt, rather than the alternative formulation of lowering the plaintiff in the estimation of right thinking members of society [para. 3.4.15]. Furthermore, there is an important conceptual difference between the tort of libel and the corresponding crime. The original policy of the law which gave rise to the creation of the offence was the prevention of breaches of the peace, rather than the the protection of individual reputations (*R. v. Holbrook* (1878)), and therefore communication of the libel to the person who is libelled can be sufficient, there being no requirement of publication to a third party. However, the danger of a breach of the peace appears to be no longer generally essential, having been replaced by the less well-defined requirement that a criminal libel must be 'serious' (*Gleaves v. Deakin* (1979)). Nevertheless, it seems that where in fact the only communication is to the person libelled, the original requirement of a danger of a breach of the peace may still be an essential element of the offence (*R. v. Adams* (1968)). It is unclear whether criminal liability can result from libelling the dead [see para. 3.4.14 for the position in tort].

3.6.04   As far as defences to a prosecution at common law are concerned, the position is as follows. If the defendant relies on the truth of the statement, he must show not only that it is in fact true, but also that its publication is for the public benefit (s. 6, Libel Act 1843). The defences of privilege [paras. 3.5.10 *et seq.*], are available here as they are in tort (*R. v. Perry* (1883)) but it is unclear whether a plea of fair comment on a matter of public interest [para. 3.5.16 *et seq.*] is available by way of defence to a prosecution (*Goldsmith v. Pressdram Ltd.* (1977)), where two reports of the judge's comments differ in this respect).

3.6.05   The statutory offence is the simpler, and may be dealt with very briefly. The publication of any libel which the defendant knows to be false, is an offence, triable at the Crown Court, and punishable with up to two years' imprisonment (s.4 of the Libel Act 1843). If the prosecution is unable to prove that the defendant knew the libel to be false, or if the facts alleged turn out to be true, the defendant may be convicted of the common law offence, whereupon he becomes liable to the statutory penalty for that offence, the maximum being imprisonment for one year (*Boaler v. R.* (1888)).

BLASPHEMY

3.7.01   Discussion of the offence of blasphemy may seem a little out of place in a chapter concerned with the law of libel, but it may conveniently be included by way of a postscript to criminal libel, because an alternative name for the offence of blasphemy is 'blasphemous libel', even though, curiously, there is no discernible overlap with the law of libel as usually understood.

3.7.02   The history of the offence of blasphemy is long and complicated, and owes a great deal to the constitutional position of the Church of England, at the head of which, of course, stands the monarch. The position in modern times, however, can be dealt with briefly.

3.7.03   Prosecutions for blasphemy are exceedingly rare, with *R v. Lemon and Gay News Ltd.* (1979) being the first example for over 60 years. The case arose from the publication in *Gay News* of a poem and an illustration describing in explicit detail acts of sodomy and fellatio on Jesus's body immediately after the crucifixion, and attributing to Jesus promiscuous homosexual practices with the apostles and others. The prosecution alleged that this amounted to 'vilification' of Jesus. Although there was no evidence that the publication would provoke any public disorder — which in previous centuries had been thought to be an essential element of the offence — the House of Lords upheld the conviction of the newspaper and its editor, on the basis that material in question had been couched in indecent or offensive terms, which were likely to shock and outrage the feelings of the general body of Christian believers in the community.

3.7.04   Although the convictions of *Gay News* and its editor may have been welcomed by many Christians, the case provoked a great deal of comment on two principal bases. First, there were those non-Christians who felt that matters which were essentially offences against God could safely to be left for Him to deal with — if, of course, He exists in the first place — and that temporal intervention is inappropriate. Secondly, and perhaps even more importantly, many people felt that in a multi-cultural society it is invidious for the law to identify one religion alone as being worthy of protection, and that logic requires all religions to be treated in the same way. Pursuing this line, the next question is whether all religions should be afforded the protection of the law, or whether none should be. The answer to this is plainly a matter for debate, but it can be argued that some religions advance such anti-social teachings that it is actually in the public interest for them to be vilified.

3.7.05   Clearly, if this argument is accepted, it leads to the conclusion that the offence of blasphemy should be abolished, and indeed abolition was the gist of the Law Commission's conclusions on the topic in 1981. Despite these conclusions, however, no legislative action ensued. It may be that Parliament was occupied with other, more urgent, business. Nevertheless, there remains a sense of injustice caused by the way in which the law protects Christian sensibilities, but not those of adherents to other faiths, as evidenced by the vehemence of the outcry from certain

Islamic quarters, in 1989, in respect of controversial references to the Prophet in Salman Rushdie's novel *The Satanic Verses*.

4 Obscene publications

4.1.01 The central concern of this chapter will be to identify, with as much precision as possible, the legal meaning of obscenity, together with a consideration of possible defences, and of the different legal procedures which are used to deal with obscene publications. There are some variations in the law according to the medium by which obscene material is purveyed. More particularly, in some respects theatrical performances and broadcasting are treated differently from printed material. However, the scope of this book is such that only the law relating to printed material will be discussed.

4.1.02 Obscenity was originally controlled exclusively by the ecclesiastical courts, but from at least the early part of the eighteenth century the common law also intervened (*R. v. Curl* (1727)). This intervention began with the recognition of an offence of obscene libel, but the modern law of obscene publications is significantly wider than that. The bulk of the modern law is to be found in the Obscene Publications Act 1959 and 1964. It even appears that s. 2(4) of the 1959 Act has abolished the common law offence of obscene libel, although the section is not explicit on the point, and in any event the House of Lords has held that the section does not prevent a conviction being recorded on a charge of *conspiracy* to publish an obscene libel (*Shaw v. Director of Public Prosecutions* (1961)).

THE MEANING OF OBSCENITY

4.2.01 Section 1(1) of the Obscene Publications Act 1959 provides:

> For the purposes of this Act an article shall be deemed to be obscene if its effect or (where the article comprises two or more distinct items) the effect of any one of its items is, if taken as a whole, such as to tend to deprave and corrupt persons who are likely, having regard

to all relevant circumstances, to read, see or hear the matter contained or embodied in it.

This has been interpreted as meaning that a significant proportion of the persons who are likely to be exposed to the material must be at risk of depravity and corruption (*R. v. Calder and Boyars Ltd.* (1968)).

4.2.02   Section 1(2) goes on to provide a very wide definition of 'article' for the purposes of the Act, namely:

Any description of article containing or embodying matter to be read or looked at or both, any sound record, and any film or other record of a picture or pictures.

Tendency to deprave and corrupt

4.2.03   The key concepts of depravity and corruption are not defined in the Obscene Publications Acts. Prosecutions will be dealt with by the Crown Court, and it will be for the jury to decide for itself whether it thinks the material in the case can be said to fall within the statutory words as they understand them in accordance with prevailing moral values. As a general proposition, the jury must undertake this task without the help of expert evidence. It seems that the only exception to this is in cases where material is directed at very young children, where expert evidence may be admissible as to the likely impact of the material upon the juvenile mind (*Director of Public Prosecutions v. A. and B.C. Chewing Gum Ltd.* (1967)).

4.2.04   In the majority of cases involving obscene publications, the material in question has been of a sexual nature. In fact, of course, the scope for human depravity is considerably wider than this might seem to suggest, and accordingly there have been cases where non-sexual material has been held to be obscene. The most famous example is *Calder (John) Publications Ltd. v. Powell* (1965), involving *Cain's Book*, by Alexander Trocchi, where the court said that a book which:

highlighted . . . the favourable effects of drug-taking . . . [raised] . . . a real danger that those into whose hands the book came might be tempted at any rate to experiment with drugs and get the favourable sensations highlighted by the book.

4.2.05   In *Calder*, the court obviously saw depravity and corruption in terms of the subsequent *conduct* of people who might read the book. However, the likelihood of depraved conduct is not necessary, as indicated by the House of Lords in *Director of Public Prosecutions v. Whyte* (1972), where it was held that there could be obscenity in the case of articles which would enable their readers to embark on purely private fantasies, unaccompanied by any overt activity of any kind. In

73

other words, depravity and corruption can exist simply as a state of mind.
4.2.06   However, s. 1(1) of the Act does not deal with a tendency to deprave and corrupt in the abstract: the tendency must exist in relation to *persons who are likely, having regard to all relevant circumstances, to read, see or hear the matter*. In the light of this, it has sometimes been argued that the only people likely to come into contact with the material in question are people who are already devotees of that kind of material anyway, and that therefore it cannot be said that they are capable of being depraved and corrupted by the material in the instant case. Ingenious though this argument is, the courts have refused to uphold it. As Lord Wilberforce said in the House of Lords in *Director of Public Prosecutions v. Whyte* (1972):

> The Act is not merely concerned with the once for all corruption of the wholly innocent, it equally protects the less innocent from further corruption, the addict from feeding or increasing his addiction.

Offences

4.2.07   There are two main offences, namely publication of an obscene article, and having an obscene article for publication, even if no publication has actually taken place. One potentially important distinction between these two very similar offences is that the first one is committed whether or not the publication is for gain, whereas it is an essential element of the second offence that the intended publication, if it takes place, shall be for gain (s. 2, of the 1959 Act).
4.2.08   *Publication* includes distribution, circulation, sale, letting on hire, giving and lending, the article in question (s. 1(3)(a) of the 1959 Act), and therefore the proprietors of libraries and the librarians employed in them, are clearly within the scope of the Act to this extent. However, it is highly unlikely that the proprietors of the vast majority of libraries, with the exception of those which are run on a commercial basis, would be held to have articles in their possession for gain. On the other hand, individual librarians, being salaried, might be considered to derive some gain, however slight, from each individual activity of their library. In practice, however, this distinction is unlikely to be significant, since liability in a library context is likely to arise only where there has been publication − otherwise no-one will know that the library possesses the article in question, and therefore there will be no complaint − and here the question of gain is irrelevant.

Defences

4.2.09   Two matters fall to be considered here. First, a defendant will be entitled to be acquitted if he shows both that he did not examine the article in question and that he had no reasonable cause to suspect that his having or publishing the article (as the case may be) would amount to an offence under s. 2 of the Act (s. 2(5) of the 1959 Act and s. 1(3)(a) of the 1964 Act). This defence should be very useful to librarians, although it is important to note that both elements of the defence must be established. Therefore the defence will not be available to a defendant who has actually examined the article but who has formed the opinion that it is not obscene.

4.2.10   Secondly, it will be a defence to prove that:

publication of the article in question is justified as being for the public good on the ground that it is in the interests of science, literature, art or learning, or of other objects of general concern (s. 4(1) of the 1959 Act).

It is also provided that:

the opinion of experts as to the literary, artistic scientific or other merits of an article may be admitted … either to establish or to negative the said ground (s. 4(2) of the 1959 Act).

4.2.11   The legislative policy underlying the defence of *public good* seems to be that the harm to individuals who are depraved and corrupted may be outweighed by wider considerations of the good of the public as a whole. At a practical level, the court is faced with an additional difficulty: having decided that the article in question has a tendency to deprave and corrupt a significant proportion of the people likely to be exposed to it, the court must then go on to identify and weigh the countervailing quantity of public good arising from the publication. However, it will be noted that on the public good issue, the court is allowed to receive expert evidence, which is, of course, in marked contrast to the position where the initial question of obscenity is being determined. Although there is little case law on the subject, the House of Lords has held that expert evidence is not admissible to show that people who are sexually repressed or deviant may benefit by using obscene publications as a vehicle for the relief of their sexual frustration, which might otherwise manifest itself in anti-social conduct (*Director of Public Prosecutions v. Jordan* (1976)). The short point is that to allow this defence in these circumstances would be to justify publication *because the material is obscene*, rather than justifying publication *despite the material's obscenity*, which is the true scope of s. 4(2).

Forfeiture of obscene articles

4.2.12   The first part of this chapter has been concerned with prosecutions in the Crown Court for offences in relation to obscene publications, but s. 3 of the Obscene Publications Act 1959, replacing s. 1 of the Obscene Publications Act 1857, also provides an alternative form of procedure, namely applications for forfeiture in the magistrates' court.

4.2.13   The essence of forfeiture proceedings under s. 3 is that someone (in practice it will almost invariably be a police officer) will swear an oath before a magistrate, to the effect that he has reasonable grounds for suspecting that obscene articles are being kept in any premises, stall or vehicle within the magistrate's area, for publication for gain. The magistrate will then issue a warrant, authorizing the police to search for and seize any articles which they believe are obscene and are being kept for publication for gain. A magistrate for the same area will then examine the articles. If he decides that they are not obscene, that will be an end of the matter and the articles will be returned. If, however, the magistrate thinks that the articles may be obscene, he will summon the occupier of the premises, stall or vehicle to come before a magistrates' court, in order to say why the articles should not be forfeited. Other people entitled to appear and argue against forfeiture are the owner, author or maker of the articles, and anyone else through whose hands they passed before they were seized. At that stage there must be a decision by the court as to whether the articles actually are obscene, but before making this decision the court must hear any arguments as to why the articles are not obscene. If these arguments succeed, the articles will be returned to the person from whom they were seized, whereas if the arguments fail, the court will order the forfeiture of the articles, which will then be destroyed by the police.

4.2.14   It must be emphasised that the onus is on the person who is summoned to show that the articles are not obscene, rather than being on the police, or anyone else, to show that they are (*Thomson v. Chain Libraries Ltd.* (1954)). However, he is required to prove his case only on the balance of probabilities, and not beyond reasonable doubt.

4.2.15   The meaning of *obscene* is the same in forfeiture proceedings as it is in prosecutions, although it will be the magistrates' court and not a jury which decides the key question of whether the material has a tendency to deprave and corrupt a significant proportion of the people who are likely to be exposed to it. The defence of *public good* is available in forfeiture proceedings as it is in prosecutions (s. 4(1) of the 1959 Act).

4.2.16   In practice, forfeiture proceedings are used more frequently than criminal proceedings, partly because proceedings in the magistrates' court are quicker and cheaper than trials in the Crown Court, and partly because they are more likely to be successful. The reasons for the greater likelihood of success are twofold. First, anyone who is opposing forfeiture has to show that the article is not obscene, and it is notoriously difficult to prove a negative. Secondly, magistrates are more likely to be case-hardened than juries, and therefore less likely to be swayed by libertarian arguments in favour of freedom of expression.

OBSCENITY, INDECENCY AND THE POSTAL SERVICE

4.3.01 Any librarian who finds himself in possession of obscene material is likely to wish to destroy it. However, come what may, the one thing he must not do with it is to send it to anyone through the post. The relevant provision is s. 11 of the Post Office Act 1953, which creates the offence of sending, attempting to send, or procuring the sending of a postal packet which contains 'any indecent or obscene article'. The offence is a serious one, and can be punished by the Crown Court with a maximum of twelve months' imprisonment.

4.3.02 It will be noted that s. 11 refers to material which is 'indecent or obscene'. This is clearly wider than 'obscene', as discussed in the earlier part of this chapter, and therefore great caution should be exercised with regard to suspect material, because merely escaping a finding of obscenity will not necessarily result in an acquittal under s. 11 of the 1953 Act.

4.3.03 Three points may be made. First, there is no requirement for any tendency to deprave and corrupt. Secondly, the test of *indecency* is an objective one, so the identity of any potential recipient is irrelevant. Thirdly, trial courts must make their decisions in the light of their own judgment and without the aid of evidence as to the meaning of *indecent*: in the words of the court in *R. v. Stamford* (1972), they are 'the custodians of the standards for the time being'.

5 Privacy, confidentiality, data protection and official secrets

5.1.01   The purpose of the law of libel and slander is, broadly, to protect people against the harmful effect of having lies told about them [chapter 3]. This leaves open the question of the law's attitude towards statements which are true but which may nevertheless be the subject of objection by the person about whom they are made. This brings up the topics of privacy, confidentiality, including the specialized area of law relating to data protection, and official secrets. This chapter will consider these topics in turn.

PRIVACY

5.2.01   'English law has not yet recognised the invasion of privacy as a tort' (*Clerk and Lindsell on Torts*, 15th edition, para. 1-48). This is in marked contradistinction to some legal systems where there are well-established bodies of principle protecting a citizen's privacy, but the fact of the matter remains that English law, despite many suggestions for reform, has not yet reached the stage where it considers the interest of privacy as such to be a sufficient justification for imposing some restrictions on the free flow of information. Nevertheless, English law does afford partial protection of privacy by means of actions for breach of confidence and the law relating to data protection. The protection of confidential material in the national interest is covered by the Official Secrets Acts, 1911 to 1989.

BREACH OF CONFIDENCE

5.3.01   In view of the moral origins of equity [paras. 1.2.04 *et seq.*], it is not surprising that the the remedy of an injunction may be available to restrain publication of information which has been obtained in confidence. The circumstances giving rise to a duty of confidentiality are varied, but will usually arise out of a contractual relationship. For example, an employee may be restrained from misusing confidential information belonging to his employer (*Thomas Marshall (Exporters) Ltd. v. Guinle* (1978)). Family relationships may also give rise to a duty of confidentiality. Thus in *Argyll v. Argyll* (1965), the court was willing to restrain one party to a celebrated divorce case from publishing material which had been obtained from the other spouse during the marriage.

5.3.02   The limits on the duty of confidentiality are extremely difficult to identify. Before leaving the topic, however, it is worth noticing *Attorney-General v. Jonathan Cape* (1975), where the court was prepared to say that publication of information obtained by a cabinet minister in his official capacity could be prohibited by injunction, although on the facts of the case the court did not feel there was any need to restrain publication of Richard Crossman's diaries relating to his time as a cabinet minister in the 1960s.

DATA PROTECTION

5.4.01   The enactment of the Data Protection Act 1984 represents what is perhaps English law's most extensive, and certainly its most coherent, incursion into the field of the protection of privacy, so an outline of its underlying principles must be provided. The Act was passed to bring English law into line with the principles contained in the Council of Europe's Convention Concerning Protection of Individuals with Regard to Automatic Processing of Personal Data, 1981.

The scope of the Data Protection Act 1984

5.4.02   The Data Protection Act 1984 creates a system of registration of data users and people who carry on computer bureaux. Perhaps the best starting point, however, is to clarify the basic terminology of the Act, namely the key terms: *data*, *personal data*, *data subject*, and *data user*.

5.4.03   *Data* is defined as:

> information recorded in a form in which it can be processed by equipment operating automatically in response to instructions given for that purpose (s. 1(2)).

In other words, manually operated systems, such as card indices and conventional filing systems, do not come within the scope of the Act .

5.4.04   *Personal data* are defined as:

> data consisting of information which relates to a living individual who can be identified from that information (or from that and other information in the possession of the data user), including any

expression of opinion about the individual but not any indication of the intentions of the data user in respect of that individual (s. 1(3)).

Thus, for example, expressions of opinion about an employee's abilities would be within the term 'personal data', whereas an expression of intention to promote − or not to promote − him to a specific post would not be.

5.4.05 *Data subject* is defined as 'an individual who is the subject of personal data' (s. 1(4)), while *data user* is defined in lengthy but reasonably self-evident terms by s. 1(5).

5.4.06 Inevitably there are a number of detailed exemptions from the provisions of the Act. Broadly speaking these fall into two categories, namely data which are trivial and non-sensitive on the one hand, and data which should be exempt on the grounds of the public interest or the interest of the data user himself.

5.4.07 The first category of trivial and non-sensitive data includes data used solely for word processing (s. 1(8)), and data concerned solely with the management of personal, family and household affairs (s. 33). A great deal of detail surrounds some of the exemptions and in practice some people may prefer to register anyway, so that they no longer have the constant worry of wondering whether they are straying beyond the bounds of the particular exemption in question. Also within the first category of exemptions are databases which are within the public domain anyway, such as computerized forms of the electoral register.

5.4.08 Turning to the second category of data, where there is some other reason for exemption, the public interest sub-category includes data held for the purposes of crime prevention and detection and the apprehension and prosecution of offenders, together with data held for the assessment and collection of taxes and duties (s. 28). The personal interest sub-category includes the power of the Secretary of State for Trade and Industry to make exemption orders in respect of the subject's right of access to information as to his own physical or mental health (s. 29(1)).

The system of registration

5.4.09 The Act creates a system under which the holder of the specifically created office of Data Protection Registrar (s. 3(1)(a)), has a duty to register both data users and people who carry on computer bureaux, provided of course that they are dealing with personal data (s. 4(1)). Section 11 gives the Registrar a power of de-registration where a registered person contravenes any of the data protection principles [para. 5.4.13]. Having created the office of Registrar, the Act also creates a body known as the Data Protection Tribunal which deals with appeals against the Registrar's decisions (s. 3(1)(b)).

Rights in relation to personal data

5.4.10 The Act gives data subjects the right of access to personal data (s. 21); the right to be compensated by the data user for damage and distress caused by inaccurate personal data (s. 22); or by the loss or unauthorized disclosure of personal data (s. 23); and rights to rectification of, and erasure of personal data from, the register (s. 24).

The data protection principles

5.4.11 The first schedule to the Act contains a statement of eight principles which are derived from the Council of Europe Convention of 1981. These principles provide the framework against which many of the Act's provisions were drafted. Additionally, s. 36(1) of the Act provides that it is the duty of the Registrar to perform his functions under the Act in such a way as to promote the observance of these principles by data users and by people carrying on computer bureaux. All the principles apply to personal data held by data users, whilst the eighth also applies to people carrying on computer bureaux.

5.4.12 The data protection principles are:

1 The information to be contained in personal data shall be obtained, and personal data shall be processed, fairly and lawfully.

2 Personal data shall be held only for one or more specified and lawful purposes.

3 Personal data held for any purpose or purposes shall not be used or disclosed in any manner incompatible with that purpose or those purposes.

4 Personal data held for any purpose or purposes shall be adequate, relevant and not excessive in relation to that purpose or those purposes.

5 Personal data shall be accurate and, where necessary, kept up to date.

6 Personal data held for any purpose or purposes shall not be kept for longer than is necessary for that purpose or those purposes.

7 An individual shall be entitled:
   (a) at reasonable intervals and without undue delay or expense:
      (i) to be informed by any data user whether he holds personal data of which that individual is the subject; and
      (ii) to access to any such data held by a data user; and
   (b) where appropriate, to have such data corrected or erased.

8 Appropriate security measures shall be taken against unauthorized access to, or alteration, disclosure or destruction of, personal data and against accidental loss or destruction of personal data.

Enforcement of the Act

5.4.13   The need to obtain registration clearly provides an opportunity for the Registrar to educate applicants as to the nature and extent of their obligations under the Act. Furthermore, the power to refuse to register an applicant, or to issue a de-registration notice to someone who is already on the register, can be seen as a means of enforcement. Additionally, the Registrar has power to issue a variety of other notices, including enforcement notices where he is satisfied that there is a breach of any of the data protection principles.

5.4.14   However, the ultimate mechanism for enforcement of the Act is provided by the creation of a range of offences, triable by either the magistrates' court or the Crown Court, and punishable by fines (s. 19). These offences, some of which are defined in terms involving a considerable amount of detail, range from basic matters such as holding personal data without being registered (s. 5(1)), and unauthorized disclosure of personal data (s. 5(2)(d)), to more minor matters such as failure to notify changes of address to the Registrar (s. 6(5)).

TRANSBORDER DATA FLOW

5.5.01   One specialized aspect of data protection arises where data are transferred between countries. This is usually called either cross-border data flow or transborder data flow, for obvious reasons. As already noted, the Data Protection Act 1984 was passed to bring English law into line with the principles contained in the Council of Europe's Convention Concerning Protection of Individuals with Regard to Automatic Processing of Personal Data, 1981 [para. 5.4.01].. It is appropriate, therefore, to consider the provisions of that Convention in relation to transborder data flow.

5.5.02   Chapter 3, article 12, of the Convention contains provisions which apply:

> to the transfer across national borders, by whatever medium, or personal data undergoing automatic processing or collected with a view to their being automatically processed.

The Convention goes on to say:

> a Party [i.e. a country which is a party to the Convention] shall not, for the sole purpose of the protection of privavcy, prohibit or subject to special authorisation, transborder flows of personal data going to the territory of another Party.

5.5.03   However, the Convention does recognize the right of each Party to depart from this principle where the law of the country from which the data originate contains elements of protection which are not present in the law of the country where the data will be received.

5.5.04　Strictly speaking, in common with all international Conventions, the Convention of 1981 does not form part of English law, but in practice the courts give serious attention to relevant Conventions when deciding how to interpret English statutes and case-law.

5.5.05　The registration provisions of the Data Protection Act 1984 require data users to identify any countries or territories outside the United Kingdom to which they intend, or may wish, to tranfer personal data (s. 4(3)(e)). It is an offence to transfer personal data without complying with s. 4(3)(e) (s. 5(2)(e)). If it is proposed to transfer data to a country which is not bound by the Convention, the Registrar has power to issue a *prohibition notice* under s. 12 (1), provided that he is satisfied that the transfer is likely to contravene, or lead to a contravention of, any of the data protection principles. Prohibition notices may also be issued where the transfer is to a country which is bound by the Convention, but the Registrar is satisfied that the person in question intends to give instructions for the further transfer of the data to a country which is not bound by the Convention. Contravention of a transfer prohibition notice is, of course, also an offence (s. 12(10)).

OFFICIAL SECRETS

5.6.01　Particular problems of confidentiality will obviously arise where national security is at stake. These problems have been addressed by a series of statutes, collectively known as the Official Secrets Acts 1911 to 1989. These Acts create several very serious offences and contain a great deal of detail. In the present context, however, it will suffice to notice the two principal types of offence under the Acts.

5.6.02　Section 1 of the 1911 Act creates a number of offences, the common core of which is that the prohibited conduct might result in some advantage, even if only indirectly, to an enemy. In other words, the offences are aimed at espionage.

5.6.03　Section 2 of the 1911 Act was a very different proposition. Broadly speaking, this section made it an offence for any civil servant, without authorization, to communicate to anyone any information which had come into his possession as a result of his work. An indication of the scope of s. 2 can be given by saying that a civil servant would be committing an offence if he went home and told his wife how many paper clips he had used at work that day. The extent to which s. 2 could be used to restrict public knowledge of governmental information, the dissemination of which might be either harmless or even beneficial to the public interest, resulted in the section being severely criticised in practically all quarters. Nevertheless, it was a peculiarly hardy specimen, and continued to flourish until the Official Secrets Act 1989 replaced it with more reasonable provisions.

5.6.04   The essence of the replacement provisions is that there will be an offence only where there is unauthorised disclosure of information which would be damaging, and the Act goes on in some detail to specify what would be considered to be damaging in various contexts.

6 Copyright and public lending right

6.1.01 The Copyright Designs and Patents Act 1988 contains a major overhaul of the law relating to copyright. However, to put the 1988 Act into perspective and to assess its likely impact, this chapter will discuss not only the provisions of that Act, but also the historical development of the law of copyright. It will conclude with a consideration of the much more recently introduced concept of Public Lending Right.

6.1.02 The basic idea underlying the law of copyright is simply that everyone is entitled to enjoy the fruits of his own labours. The plain justice of this is probably so obvious that few people would seek to dispute it. A homely attempt to explain why the law of copyright has developed may be found in the Report of a Committee which was set up to consider the Law on Copyright and Designs (Cmnd. 6732) (usually known as the Whitford Committee because its chairman was Whitford J., a High Court judge):

> If rival bakers bake bread, each one does his work and makes his profit without helping himself to the product of the skill and labour of his rival ... it has long been recognised that only the original author ought to have the right to reproduce the original article and sell the copies thus reproduced. If other people were free to do this they would be making a profit out of the skill and labour of the original author.

6.1.03 Of course, copyright now protects not only writers, but also composers, designers, publishers and others who rely on their skills in a creative sphere.

THE HISTORICAL DEVELOPMENT OF COPYRIGHT

6.2.01 The major provisions of the Copyright, Designs and Patents Act 1988 came into force in 1989 but some of the effects of the Act will not be fully felt until it has been operational for some time and a body of case law has developed.

6.2.02 Although there have been statutes dealing with the law of copyright since the eighteenth century, it seems that the common law recognized the existence of copyright even before that. It would appear from references made in earlier cases that, as a matter of custom, members of the book trade had been entitled to exclusive rights in the works which they published. Such a system operated reasonably successfully while the book trade remained a small and easily controlled entity, but, by the beginning of the eighteenth century, literacy was spreading, and the greater demand for the written word brought with it a much larger publishing industry. One consequence of this was a need for more effective methods of control to protect the position of the author and, as a result, the Copyright Act 1709 (also known as the Statute of Anne) was enacted.

6.2.03 Briefly, the effect of the Act of 1709 was to give the author of a book a period of 14 years within which he had an exclusive right either to print it himself or to assign his rights and authorize someone else to publish it on his behalf, with more limited rights for a further period of 14 years. To ensure that a book was protected in this way, its title had to be registered at Stationers' Hall in London before the first publication. If there was no registration, there was no protection.

6.2.04 The Act of 1709 dealt essentially with books, but it became apparent that there was a need to protect other areas of creative endeavour, and in 1833 the Dramatic Copyright Act was passed. This Act gave the author of a work of entertainment—that is, a play or a musical piece—the right to present it to the public. The right extended for a period of 28 years or for the life of the author, whichever was the longer.

6.2.05 There followed a number of Acts which extended protection to further spheres of activity and, during the nineteenth century, a degree of international cooperation enabled the signing of a Convention by a number of mainly European states which conferred the protection of copyright in the territory of each signatory on works which were first published in the territory of any of the other signatories.

6.2.06 This piecemeal development of the legislation continued until the enactment of the Copyright Act 1911. The 1911 Act was essentially a consolidating statute which took some 20 earlier pieces of legislation into account. The significance of the Act was that, for the first time, combined protection was given to 'original literary, dramatic and musical works'. Prior to this, for example, an author of a book had no protection if his book was used as the basis of a play or an opera.

6.2.07 The next landmark was the publication of the Gregory Report on Copyright (Cmnd.8662), which led to the enactment of the Copyright

Act 1956. Part of the purpose of the 1956 Act was to take into account a variety of international developments, including most importantly, the Universal Copyright Convention of 1952. Nevertheless, until the 1988 Act, some of the provisions of another major international agreement, the Berne Copyright Convention of 1886, which was last ratified in 1971 by some 60 member countries, had still not been incorporated into English law. Just as the 1956 Act had been an updating statute in its day, so the Copyright, Designs and Patents Act 1988 represents a further measure of updating. Some aspects of both these Acts must now be considered in more detail.

The Copyright Act 1956

6.2.08 The 1956 Act dealt not only with literary, dramatic and musical works, but also with industrial designs, films, sound recordings, broadcasts and television. The Act was divided into six parts, the most important being Parts I and II, covering copyright in original works and copyright in the field of sound recordings and broadcasts. Since 1956 various technological advances, including the introduction of video recorders and rapid spread of computers, have led to a number of amending Acts in an attempt to ensure that the legislation has kept up to date with current needs.

6.2.09 Nevertheless, over the years the copyright legislation was extensively criticized and, in 1973, the Whitford Committee was established, with instructions to 'consider the law on copyright and designs'. The Committee's detailed terms of reference were very wide, covering many technical design areas and accordingly its recommendations were extensive.

6.2.10 So far as copyright was concerned, the recommendations were mainly restricted to clarifying the somewhat muddy waters of the law in areas where either the application of the existing legislation had proved to be uncertain, or the Act simply did not apply at all. In particular, the piecemeal development of the legislation through the introduction of various amending statutes meant that it was increasingly difficult, especially for the layman, to ascertain exactly what the law was. The Committee also considered that the rights of employees, many of whom were in a position where they created works which could potentially be subject to copyright, should be defined more clearly. The Committee was also concerned about the control over the reproduction of works and suggested that a system of licensing should be established, as well as a Tribunal to oversee the operation of the legislation. This Tribunal would also be empowered to authorize the infringement of copyright in circumstances where the owner could not be traced.

6.2.11 In 1981 the Whitford Committee's report was followed by a

Green Paper (Cmnd. 8302), entitled *Reform of the Law Relating to Copyright, Designs and Performers' Protection*, which in turn was followed, in 1986, by a White Paper (Cmnd. 9712) called *Intellectual Property and Innovation*.

6.2.12   The distinction between a Green Paper and a White Paper was explained by the former prime Minister, Sir Harold Wilson, in his book *The Labour Government 1964-71*:

> A White Paper is essentially a statement of government policy in such terms that withdrawal or major amendment ... tends to be regarded as a humiliating withdrawal. A Green Paper represents the best that the Government can propose on the given issue, but, remaining uncommitted, it is able without loss of face to leave its final decision open until it has been able to consider public reaction to it.

In other words, Green Papers are consultative documents, whereas White Papers contain specific legislative proposals.

6.2.13   Although not all legislation is preceded by Green Papers and White Papers, they frequently act as forerunners to the introduction of legislation and, in this instance, they culminated in the passage of the Copyright, Designs and Patents Act 1988. The long title of the Act describes it as being, *inter alia*, 'an Act to restate the law of copyright'.

THE COPYRIGHT, DESIGNS AND PATENTS ACT 1988

6.3.01   The Copyright, Designs and Patents Act 1988 received the Royal Assent on 15 November 1988. Although it is possible for an Act of Parliament to come into force on the day that the Royal Assent is given, it is more common for a future date to be fixed either by the Act itself or by the appropriate Secretary of State. In the case of almost all the provisions of the 1988 Act, the last alternative has been adopted. There may be various advantages in this method of bringing statutes into force. For example, the people most likely to be affected by the new legislation are given some opportunity of adapting to it, and the precise date of implementation can be fixed with regard to the progress of administrative arrangements such as the making of regulations under the Act.

6.3.02   The 1988 Act is bulky, being divided into seven Parts and running to 306 sections. However, it is the first and largest Part which is of major interest to librarians. The remainder of the Act concentrates on rights in performances, design, and patents. The Act repeals the Copyright Act 1956 in its entirety, as well as the Copyright (Amendment) Acts of 1982 and 1983 and the Copyright (Computer Software) Amendment Act 1985. The implementation of Part I of the 1988 Act was delayed until 1 August 1989, by which time both the Copyright

(Librarians and Archivists) (Copying of Copyright Material) Regulations 1989, and the Copyright (Educational Establishments) (No. 2) Order 1989 (S.I. 1989, No. 1068) had been made. Both the Regulations and the Order also came into force on 1 August 1989.

The nature of copyright

6.3.03 'Copyright' is defined in section 1 of the 1988 Act as a property right which exists in

(a) original literary, dramatic, musical or artistic works;
(b) sound recordings, films, broadcasts or cable programmes, and
(c) the typographical arrangement of published editions.

The Act specifically includes a computer program within the definition of a 'literary work' (s. 3(1)(b)).

6.3.04 It is important to emphasize that the protection of copyright extends only to ideas which are *written down or otherwise recorded*. Thus the Act confers no protection on ideas, until they have been *permanently* documented in some way: verbal publication to other people is not enough. (Whether the law offers any protection other than through copyright will, of course, depend on all the circumstances. For breach of confidence, for example, see chapter 5.)

6.3.05 On the other hand, the Act does not confine itself to works which have literary or dramatic merit. The courts have held a multitude of things to be literary works for the purposes of copyright protection, including such apparently unliterary material as lists of football fixtures (*Football League Ltd. v. Littlewoods Pools Ltd.* (1959)). 'Dramatic' and 'musical' works have been given an equally wide interpretation, although lyrics are included as literary and not musical works.

6.3.06 A work is only protected by the Act if it is original. However, in this context the word 'original' is used in a rather technical sense. More particularly, there is no requirement that the work must necessarily be new, but simply that it must be 'original' to the author in the sense that it consists substantially of his own work. For example, all street maps of a given area must be identical if they are to be accurate. In such cases the requirement of originality will not operate to preclude the law of copyright from covering the layout and presentation of the material.

6.3.07 As far as the title of a book or other work is concerned, the position is that copyright protection will exist only in the relatively rare case of a title which is so long, or so complicated, that it can be said to be the product of the application of skill and labour. However, this does not mean that no legal protection whatsoever is available in more ordinary cases: the tort known as 'passing off' may be relevant. Briefly, the essence of passing off is that if one trader passes off his goods or services as being the goods or services of another trader, he commits the tort. More fully, according to Lord Diplock in *Erven Warnink v. J. Townend & Sons (Hull) Ltd.* (1979), there must be:

> (1) a misrepresentation, (2) made by a trader in the course of trade, (3) to prospective customers of his, or ultimate consumers of goods and services supplied by him, (4) which is calculated to injure the business or goodwill of another trader (in the sense that this is a reasonable consequence), and (5) which causes actual damage to a business or goodwill of the trader by whom the action is brought, or ... will probably do so.

6.3.08   There are many cases in which titles have been held to be protected by the tort of passing off, but the decision facing the court is by no means always an easy one. In particular, the more purely descriptive a title is, the more difficult it will be to invoke the protection of the law, since otherwise, for example, there could only be one text book called *The Law of Contract*.

6.3.09   Anthologies represent an interesting problem for the law of copyright. To the extent that anthologies consist of a number of original works, reproduced either in whole or in part, and which are then assembled and presented together as a book, it could be argued that they contain no originality. Of course, it is true that each individual author will own the copyright in his work, and the anthologist will need to obtain the consent of each author before reproducing his work. But the anthologist himself will have used his own skill and judgment, and expended his own energy, in selecting and arranging the material which he has anthologized, and therefore the anthology will also be an original work in its own right, with its own copyright protection. Finally, it may be noted that there is an exception to the principle that anthologizing amounts to a breach of copyright in the works which are anthologized. The exception relates only to anthologies prepared solely for educational use and which are comprised mainly of material which has no copyright. In this instance, copyright in the balance of the material is not infringed provided that a number of conditions are satisfied, principal among which is a requirement for the original authorship to be acknowledged.

Moral rights

6.3.10   For the first time in the history of the English law of copyright, the 1988 Act incorporates provisions to protect what have become known as an author's 'moral rights'. These rights have been recognized internationally for some time in accordance with the Berne Copyright Convention, and Chapter 4 of the 1988 Act, consisting of ss. 77 – 89, extends this recognition to English law. Basically, these moral rights cover four matters.

6.3.11 First, there is the right to be identified as the author of the work on any publication or public performance of any work (ss. 77–79). Secondly, there is the right to object to any derogatory treatment of the work, such as a cinematic adaptation of a novel (ss. 80–83). Thirdly, there is the right not to have a work falsely attributed (s. 84). A version of this right was introduced by s. 43 of the 1956 Act, but it was subject to certain limitations which restricted its utility, and the new version is intended to be an improvement. Fourthly, in regard to private photographs and films, there is a right to privacy (s. 85).

6.3.12 Of course, the author can waive these rights (s. 87). Any waiver would usually be express, but the possibility of implied waiver is clearly envisaged by a provision to the effect that when copyright in a work has been assigned or licensed [para.6.3.20], the author must specifically request in writing that he continues to be identified as the author.

6.3.13 According to s. 80 of the Act, derogatory treatment means some kind of adaptation or rearrangement of a work in such a way as to prejudice the honour or reputation of the author. In this context, as in the context of defamation [chapter 3], any assessment of what is 'prejudicial' is likely to be very subjective, but, in copyright cases, unlike defamation cases, the judge will simply have to do his best, since it is not the practice to have jury trials in these cases. Although this may mean that some decisions of the courts may be out of line with the views of the man in the street, it does have the advantage of being likely to promote consistency of decisions.

6.3.14 Under the Copyright Act 1956 the plaintiff had a right of action where his work was wrongly attributed to someone else. This principle has been restated and developed by s. 84 of the 1988 Act, under the heading of 'false attribution'. The concept is well-illustrated by the case of *Moore v. News of the World* (1972). The plaintiff in this case, Mrs. Moore, was a popular singer of the time and was more widely known by her professional name of Dorothy Squires. She was married to Roger Moore, a popular actor who gained a certain degree of celebrity from playing a character known as Simon Templar (or 'the Saint') in a television series.

6.3.15 The plaintiff gave an interview to a reporter from the defendant newspaper. The article which subsequently appeared in the newspaper was written in the first person and was headlined 'How my love for the Saint went sour by Dorothy Squires'. In smaller print appeared the words 'talking to Weston Taylor'. The plaintiff disputed the contents of the article which she had not seen prior to its publication. Furthermore, she alleged that the method of presentation implied that she had written the article herself. The Court of Appeal agreed with her, holding that writing the article in the first person amounted to falsely attributing the article to her. She was awarded damages of £100 in respect of the false attribution, although it is interesting to note that she also brought a libel action against the same newspaper in respect of the same story, for which she received damages amounting to £4,300.

6.3.16 There are exceptions to the moral rights provisions. For example, an author who is employed by a newspaper cannot object under the Act if he creates his work expressly for the purpose of publication in the newspaper and, after submission, the work is adapted or edited in a derogatory way. Any dispute arising in this area will more properly be dealt with in the legal context of his contract of employment, rather than under the law of copyright and its derivatives.

6.3.17 Section 85 confers rights of privacy in relation to photographs and films taken for private and domestic purposes. The immediate impetus behind the enactment of this provision was the abolition, by s. 4(3) of the Act, of the former principle that copyright in commissioned photographs belonged to the commissioner, rather than to the photographer. Clearly, the abolition of this principle, without the substitution of anything else, would leave the people who appear in photographs powerless to control the reproduction of those photographs. It follows that, in practice, s. 85 is most likely to benefit those members of society whose personal activities are a source of constant interest to certain sectors of the public. However, section 85(2) does state that there is an exception to the right when the the photograph or film is included 'incidentally' in an artistic work, film, broadcast or cable programme. The Act gives no guidance as to the meaning of 'incidental' in this context, but no doubt case-law will clarify the matter in due course.

6.3.18 An infringement of a moral right will be treated by the court as a breach of statutory duty owed by the infringer to the person entitled to the right. This means that the infringer can be sued and damages can be awarded against him by way of compensation to the wronged party. The Act also provides that the court may additionally grant an injunction to prevent continued infringement, or order that a disclaimer is issued dissociating the name of the author from the adaptation of the work.

Who benefits from copyright?

6.3.19 The first owner of the copyright is the author, even if the work is first *recorded in permanent form* by someone else. In other words, it is generally the *creator* of the work who obtains the benefit of the protection provided by the Act. It is interesting to see a new provision introduced by the Act which attempts to provide protection for works which may be produced and created by computers (described as *computer-generated works*). This provision ascribes authorship of these to the person who effectively puts together the program which brings about the creation of the work (s. 9(3)), and is an attempt to anticipate a situation in the future whereby a computer can, from information fed to it, create its own original works.

6.3.20 It follows from the basic proposition that copyright is a property right, and that the original owner has similar powers to deal with it as any other owner has in respect of any other type of property. Thus, the author has the power to assign his rights in his work (in other words, to transfer his rights to another person), or to grant a licence to enable someone else to do certain expressly stated things with the work. He may, for example, grant a limited right to publish for a short time, or allow part of his work to be adapted in a particular way. Assignment would normally allow the assignee to have full rights in the work, whereas a licence would be more restrictive. Joint authors are jointly entitled to the benefit of the Act and the consent of both, or all, of them is required before any assignment or licence of the copyright can be effected. This does not apply quite so strictly in cases where each party prepared separate and easily divisible parts of the work, because then it is possible for copyright in one part to be assigned independently of the other.

6.3.21 A copyright owner may also leave the benefit of his copyright to another person by his will, or it may pass on his intestacy. Although the death of any copyright owner results in copyright passing to someone else, a particularly famous example is provided by the will of J.M. Barrie, who left the rights in *Peter Pan* to the Great Ormond Street Hospital for Sick Children [see also para. 6.3.31].

6.3.22 'Moral rights' cannot be assigned although they can be left by will and they can pass on intestacy (ss. 94 and 95).

6.3.23 Sometimes difficulties arise in connection with identifying the copyright owner. This problem is particularly acute when the author produces the work during the course of his employment. In those circumstances, it is usual for the copyright to be owned by the employer (s. 11 of the Act), at least in those cases where the employer makes use of the work, although argument can always be made as to what is meant by 'in the course of one's employment'.

6.3.24 In the rather complex case of *Beloff v. Pressdram Ltd. and Another* (1973) the facts were, briefly, that a member of the staff of the *Observer* newspaper, who was the plaintiff, wrote a memorandum which was distributed to the editorial staff. The contents of the memorandum were 'leaked' to a contributor to the satirical magazine *Private Eye* and were subsequently printed in full in an article in *Private Eye*. The editor of the *Observer* purported to assign any copyright which it might have in the memorandum to the plaintiff who then brought an action for breach of copyright. The plaintiff's claim failed on the basis that the editor had no authority to assign the copyright and, as on the facts of the case the plaintiff was obviously an employee rather than a freelance, the original copyright remained with the *Observer*. In other words, the newspaper itself should have brought the action.

6.3.25 Situations like this do, of course, ultimately rest on what has been agreed, either expressly or impliedly, between the employer and the employee. For example, it may well be that an architect will specifically agree with his client that he shall retain the copyright in his drawings. Alternatively, if the client acquires the copyright, a significantly higher fee will usually be negotiated.

6.3.26 In addition to the originator's copyright, publishers are entitled to the copyright contained in every published edition of a work, thus protecting the particular form and layout of the publication.

The nature of the benefit conferred by the 1988 Act

6.3.27 First, it must be remembered that copyright protection commences as soon as the work is created and recorded. More specifically, the work does not have to be published.

6.3.28 The word 'copyright' itself clearly indicates that the copyright owner has the exclusive right to copy the work. In addition, the Act provides that he also has exclusive rights to issue copies of the work to the public, to perform, show or play the work in public, to broadcast the work or include it in a cable programme service, and to make an adaptation of the work or do any of the above things in relation to an adaptation (s. 16). It follows, therefore, that any other person, who does any of these things without the licence or consent of the owner, is infringing the owner's copyright. It is interesting to note that, as part of the updating process, the Act creates a new 'rental right' in relation to renting sound recordings, films and computer programs to the public (s. 18).

6.3.29 Copyright can be infringed even though the whole of a work is not copied: the Act refers to the use of a 'substantial part'. Although this may sound like a purely quantitative test, case law has established that a 'substantial part' has to be judged with regard to its quality rather than its quantity. For example, in *Francis Day & Hunter Ltd. v. Bron* (1963), it was decided that copyright can be infringed when a few bars of a lyric are copied, if those few bars form an essential part of the original work. In many cases the opening words of a song or poem may be memorable, and these will be worthy of protection even though they form only a small part of the whole.

6.3.30 Parodies pose a particular problem in this context. In the case of *Joy Music Ltd. v. Sunday Pictorial Newspapers (1920) Ltd.* (1960), dealing with a parody of a popular song, McNair J. said that the question for the court was whether the defendant, who was the parodist, had bestowed such mental labour on the work he had taken and subjected it to such revision and alteration that he had produced an original work. This case is also authority for the proposition that what constitutes a 'substantial part' is a question of fact for the court on each occasion, and that there can be no hard and fast guidelines.

The duration of copyright

6.3.31 Basically, copyright protection lasts for 50 years from the date of the author's death, or, in the case of joint authors, the death of the last survivor (s. 12). In this context it is interesting to note that the Act contains specific and unique provisions in favour of the Great Ormond Street Hospital for Sick Children. The problem was that the hospital's period of benefit from the rights in *Peter Pan* expired on 31 December 1987, 50 years from the date of the author's death. The financial consequences for the hospital were likely to be so serious that the Act created a unique right for the hospital to continue to receive royalties even though the copyright had expired (s. 301 and Schedule 6). This is one of the few provisions of the Act which came into force virtually immediately [see, also, para 6.3.21].

6.3.32 ther exceptions to the basic rule apply to anonymous works, where copyright protection attaches to the work itself, and lasts for 50 years from the end of the year of first publication, unless, of course, the identity of the creator becomes known, in which case the usual rule applies (s. 12). Similarly, with sound recordings or films, the 50-year period is calculated from the end of the year in which the film or recording was first released to the public (s. 13). A publisher's copyright, which consists of the copyright in the typographical arrangement of the work, runs for only 25 years, from the end of the year in which the work was first published (s. 15). Copyright in a work made by a Crown servant in the course of his duties, known as *Crown copyright*, exists for 125 years from the end of the calendar year in which the work was made, except that if the work is commercially published within 75 years from the end of the year in which it was made, Crown copyright exists for 50 years from the end of the year in which it was published (s. 163). In the case of Acts of Parliament, copyright exists for 50 years from the end of the calendar year in which the Royal Assent was given (s. 164). Her Majesty's Stationery Office issues advice on copying material protected by Crown and Parliamentary copyright. From time to time, all Chief Librarians receive information as to the general consents which are currently in force, and in respect of which neither prior request nor any payment is required. (Appendix B reproduces the current consents.)

6.3.33 The rights, listed in paragraph 6.3.28, and referred to by the heading to s. 16 as 'acts restricted by copyright', show that the Parliamentary draftsman had a refreshing awareness of both traditional and contemporary means of communication. Thus s. 21(4) provides that a 'translation' of a computer program from one computer language to another is an adaptation which is restricted by the Act, whilst s. 19(2)(a) includes a provision that incorporating copyright material into a sermon can amount to an infringement.

Remedies for infringement of copyright

6.3.34   The provisions of the Act dealing with remedies for infringment of copyright depend on a distinction between 'primary infringement', which consists of doing any of the acts prohibited by s. 16, and 'secondary infringement', which consists of 'dealing' with infringing copies: for example, importing books which have been published in breach of copyright. Basically, the importance of the distinction between primary and secondary infringement is that the former is within the realm of civil law, whereas the latter is within the realm of criminal law.

6.3.35   As primary infringement is a matter of civil law, an owner whose copyright has been infringed will normally seek one or more of either damages, to compensate him for the loss he has suffered from the infringement, or an account of profits, or an injunction to prevent future infringements. Section 97 does, however, specify that the innocent defendant, or in other words, someone who did not know and had no reason to believe that he was acting in breach of copyright, cannot have damages awarded against him. This defence is specifically limited to claims for damages, and it would not prevent the copyright owner from obtaining an injunction to prevent further infringement, if the court considers that such an order would be fair and reasonable in all the circumstances of the case, nor does it prevent the copyright owner from asking the court to order the infringer to account to him for any profit which he has already made from the infringement. Obviously, this remedy of an account can produce substantial compensation where the pirating of the work has been successful, but even without a specific application for an account, s. 97(2) provides that when assessing damages the court must consider both the 'flagrancy' of the infringement and any benefit which the defendant obtained as a result.

6.3.36   The conceptual difference between an order for damages and an order for an account is two-fold. First, damages are designed to compensate the plaintiff for his loss, so the court has to decide how much he would have made if there had been no infringement, and this will not necessarily be the same as the the amount which the infringer actually made. Secondly, damages are a remedy at common law, and therefore the plaintiff is entitled to them once he has proved the facts necessary to establish his claim, whereas an account is an equitable remedy, which means that ultimately the court has a discretion as to whether to grant or withhold it. This discretion is not, of course, exercised capriciously, but in accordance with the principles outlined in para. 1.6.11 *et seq.*

6.3.37   Secondary infringement is a criminal offence. The penalties prescribed by the Act vary according to the precise form in which the offence is committed, but the maxima include imprisonment for two years and/or a fine, which is not limited by the Act, and which may, therefore, be of any amount the court thinks fit, provided, of course, that the established principles of sentencing are applied.

6.3.38   It will be remembered that in a case of primary infringement, liability for infringement is generally absolute, with the infringer's knowledge or lack of knowledge being relevant only in relation to the order which the court chooses to make [para.6.3.35]. In a case of secondary infringement, however, s. 107 provides that the infringer can be convicted only if he either *knows*, or has *reason to believe*, that he is dealing with an infringing copy.

Licensing schemes and the copyright tribunal

6.3.39   Copyright owners can become members of licensing schemes, whereby a group of owners get together to establish one body which then has the responsiblity for issuing licences covering a number of different works. The advantage of this to the owner, and to the licensee, is that it relieves him of the administrative headache of discussing and arranging the licence with possibly the need to contact a number of different copyright owners. Conceivably, a potential licensee who wished to adapt a book to produce a film would need a licence from the author of the book, his publisher and the composer of the film's introductory music. The disadvantage for the licensee, however, is that the group has more negotiating power than an individual which can lead to a monopolistic situation.

6.3.40   Under the 1956 Act, a tribunal named the Performing Rights Tribunal, was established to control and adjudicate in disputes which arose over the licensing of public performances. This, of course, included broadcasting and cable programmes. The 1988 Act renames it the Copyright Tribunal and extends its powers so that it covers all licensing bodies which are set up to negotiate any kind of copyright licence. The Tribunal consists of a chairman and two deputy chairmen, all of whom must be legally qualified and are appointed by the Lord Chancellor. They will be assisted by between two and eight lay members. The Tribunal has a number of functions and miscellaneous powers, the most important of which is to prevent the establishment of societies which exert undue control over licensing. The Tribunal will be able to control the level of charges made for licences under licensing schemes and prevent them becoming unduly onerous. Licensing bodies will also be able to submit their scheme to the Tribunal for advance approval. Once a scheme has been approved by the Tribunal, a person who complies with the terms of the scheme — by paying the requisite fee and complying with the conditions — will not need a formal licence in order to escape the restrictions of the Act, he will be treated as if had a licence. Furthermore, where the licensing scheme is not specific as to the works which are covered by it and a licensee infringes copyright in the belief that he is complying with a scheme, the operator of the scheme must indemnify the licensee against any liability which he might incur, provided that the licensee has genuine grounds for his belief.

6.3.41   Under the 1988 Act, a person may apply to the Tribunal if he feels that he has been unreasonably refused a licence or that he has been granted a licence and that its terms are unreasonably onerous. The Tribunal can then, if it feels that the applicant has a genuine claim, make an order to the effect that a licence must be granted to comply with terms laid down by it. When adjudicating on these disputes the Tribunal does not have a completely free hand. It must take into consideration various matters which are specified in the Act. For example, if an application is referred to the Tribunal in respect of a licence to permit reprographic copying, the Tribunal must take into account the extent to which the work is generally available, the proportion of the work to be copied and the type of use to which the copied work is to be put (s. 130). Applications can also be made in respect of licences which are about to expire to enable them to be extended.

6.3.42   The Tribunal is the kind of body whose decision-making processes will be subject to judicial review. Additionally, s. 152 provides that an appeal on a point of law will lie from the Tribunal to the High Court. [The distinction between *review* and *appeal* is explained in para. 2.3.20.]

6.3.43   One aspect of the Tribunal's function is to encourage the operation of licensing schemes. It will obviously be appropriate for such schemes to be set up in relation to reprographic and other copying facilities used in public libraries and elsewhere. Such use of licensing schemes for copying would certainly clarify the law in this area and avoid the existing ever-present risk of infringement of copyright. Furthermore, the Act anticipates that schemes will be established to make particular provision for the reproduction of material by educational establishments. The Secretary of State is given the power to widen the scope of these schemes to include additional material where he believes that works have been unreasonably excluded and inclusion would not prejudice the interests of the copyright owner.

Activities which are permitted in relation to copyright works: the general exceptions

6.3.44   Obviously it would be totally impracticable for the law to seek to prevent all copying of all work protected by copyright, and therefore various activities are allowed without infringing copyright. The topic of activities which are permitted can be divided between those activities which are permitted generally, and those which are permitted specifically in the context of libraries. It will be convenient to deal with generally permitted activities first, and then to proceed to a more detailed examination of the activities which are specifically permitted in the library context.

6.3.45   'Fair dealing' is a phrase which is often used loosely to describe a range of situations where someone appears to be infringing copyright, but is not actually doing so, because the activity has the protection of the Act. Technically, however, the Act applies the label of 'fair dealing' only to the activities covered by ss. 29 and 30, but there is no doubt that the idea of fairness as between copyright owners and the public at large, lies behind a variety of other sections of the Act which permit certain activities.

6.3.46   Taking the technical meaning of 'fair dealing' first, and at the risk of stating the obvious, the idea is simply that certain types of activity are fair and reasonable in themselves, and do either no harm, or at worst no significant harm, to copyright owners. The Act provides that fair dealing for the purposes of making of copies in connection with research and private study will not infringe copyright (s. 29). Similarly, fair dealing for the purposes of criticism or review, or the reporting of current events will not amount to an infringment, *provided that* there is an acknowledgement of the original work (s. 30).

6.3.47   The meaning of 'fair dealing' cannot be specified with any degree of precision, but case law can be used to provide some guidelines. The case of *Hubbard and Another v. Vosper and Another* (1972) is a leading example. The facts concerned the Church of Scientology of California, whose founder, Hubbard, had written a number of books and pamphlets expounding the doctrine which he termed Scientology. Vosper, having been a member of the cult for 14 years, during which time he had had access to the cult's literature, much of which was confidential to the members, subsequently became disillusioned and left the cult. He wrote a book about Scientology which was highly critical of the cult and which contained extensive extracts from Hubbard's writings. Hubbard sought an injunction to prevent publication of the book. In situations of this sort, the plaintiff applies for an interim injunction (known technically as an 'interlocutory injunction'), on an emergency basis, to try to stop the alleged harm from happening, rather than waiting until after the event and simply claiming damages to cover his loss. The procedure is that the court hears the emergency application with a brief resumé of the alleged facts, and submissions as to the law, and then decides whether or not it should grant an injunction pending the full trial. When deciding whether an interlocutory injunction was appropriate in the present case, Lord Denning M.R. said, in the Court of Appeal:

> It is impossible to define what is fair dealing. It must be a question of degree. You must consider first the number and extent of the quotations and extracts. Are they altogether too many and too long to be fair? Then you must consider the use made of them. If they are used as a basis for comment, criticism or review that may be a fair dealing. If they are used to convey the same information as the author, for a rival purpose, that may be unfair ... But after all is said and done it must be a matter of impression. As with fair comment in the law of libel, so with fair dealing in the law of copyright. The tribunal of fact must decide. In the present case, there is material on which the tribunal of fact could find this to be a fair dealing.

6.3.48   The court will not grant an interlocutory injunction if it believes that the defendant has an adequate defence. Thus in *Hubbard's* case the Court of Appeal refused to grant the injunction on the basis that Vosper's use of the extracts could, perhaps, be justified as fair dealing for the purpose of criticism and review. Furthermore, the Court held that this included criticism of the underlying doctrine of the cult. The case also clearly shows the importance of the facts in each case and demonstrates a parallel with the law of libel. The publication of an allegedly libellous book will not normally be restrained if the defendant can plausibly plead the defence of justification. Similarly, in copyright cases, an interlocutory injunction will not normally be granted to restrain publication if the defendant can plausibly plead the defence of fair dealing.

6.3.49   At a more practical level, the Society of Authors publishes guidelines for the benefit of its members, indicating what the Society thinks may constitute a 'substantial part' of a copyright work. Whilst urging members always to ask permission whenever there is any doubt, the Society's Quick Guide No. 10 says:

> A few sentences taken from a long novel or biography are unlikely to be a 'substantial part' of the original work, but a few lines of poetry may be.

6.3.50   Turning to areas which are not technically within the meaning of 'fair dealing', but which can conveniently be considered at this juncture, the first point is that there is no infringement if a work is included 'incidentally' in a sound recording, broadcast or other such programme (s. 31). Although the Act does not explain what is meant by 'incidental' in this context, the general idea is quite plain. For example, without this provision, a television director whose sets included copyright paintings hanging on the wall, might be at risk of an action brought by the painter.

6.3.51 Secondly, people involved in education benefit quite extensively from detailed exceptions contained in the Act (ss. 32–36). The relevant provisions are complex. For example, both teachers and students are specifically allowed to make copies, subject to an exception which generally excludes reprographic copying (s. 32(1)). However, this exception is itself subject to exceptions, notable among which is that reprographic copying is specifically permitted, provided that not more than 1 per cent of any work is copied by or on behalf of any establishment within any one quarter (1 January to 31 March, and so on) (s. 36(2)), and provided also that no licences are available which would permit the copying (s. 36(3)). Additionally, of course, students may well fall within the private study exception [para. 6.3.46].

6.3.52 The Act does not require copying to take place in an educational establishment, so teachers and students could use public library copying facilities and still fall within the exceptions outlined in the previous paragraph [the copyright provisions specifically relating to libraries are discussed at paras. 6.3.55 *et seq.*]

6.3.53 Finally, in relation to education, it seems to be likely that a large proportion of copying will be done in accordance with licensing schemes, and therefore s. 36 will probably be little used.

6.3.54 Thirdly, there is an obvious public interest in the easy availability of certain types of material. The Act, therefore, contains detailed exceptions in relation to parliamentary proceedings, Royal Commissions, court proceedings and potential infringement in the course of the performance of a statutory duty (ss. 45–50). Local authorities, for example, are obliged to make various documents available to the public. Inevitably, these documents are copied to enable members of the public to inspect and study them. As public libraries are part of the local government service, this would apply equally to them, since it would be unrealistic for compliance with such a statutory duty to lead to the local authority being in breach of copyright.

Activities which are permitted in relation to copyright works: the library exceptions

6.3.55 Sections 37–44 of the Act specifically apply to libraries and librarians. Additionally, the Act enables the Secretary of State for Trade and Industry to make delegated legislation to supplement the Act itself, subject to certain specified guidelines. By way of exercise of these powers, the Secretary of State has made the Copyright (Librarians and

Archivists) (Copying of Copyright Material) Regulations 1989 (S.I. 1989 No. 1212), replacing the Copyright (Libraries) Regulations 1957 which were in existence under the 1956 Act. (As their title suggests, the 1989 Regulations contain material of interest to archivists as well as to librarians, but only the latter will be dealt with here, in view of the scope of this book.) The Copyright (Educational Establishments) (No. 2) Order 1989 (S.I. 1989 No. 1068), is also relevant. Both the 1989 Regulations and the 1989 Order came into force on 1 August 1989, and must be read together with the 1988 Act if the law as a whole is to be understood.

6.3.56   As a starting point, it is necessary to note that the concept of a *prescribed library* is central to this part of the legislation. The meaning of a *prescribed library* varies according the context, with the possibilities being as follows. First, ss. 38 and 39 of the Act, dealing with the copying of published work for the purposes of research or private study [para. 6.3.46], apply only to libraries which are administered by public library authorities, school libraries and other libraries attached to educational establishments (including universities and other institutions of further and higher education), certain specified libraries (namely the British Library, the National Library of Wales, the National Library of Scotland, the Bodleian Library, Oxford, and the University Library, Cambridge), parliamentary libraries and libraries of government departments, and any other library in the United Kingdom which is established to facilitate or encourage the study of bibliography, education, fine arts, history, languages, law, literature, medicine, music, philosophy, religion, science (including natural and social science) and technology (Part A of Schedule 1 to the 1989 Regulations). Not unreasonably, profit-making libraries are *not* prescribed and therefore they do not have the benefit of the Act. Libraries which are attached to other organization are only protected by the Act if the other organization is non-profit making. Thus, for example, a church library would have the benefit of the Act, whilst a library in a solicitor's office would not.

6.3.57   For the purposes of sections 41−43 of the Act, dealing with copying for the purposes of preserving or replacing published material, or copying unpublished material for the purposes of research or private study [para. 6.3.46], all libraries in the United Kingdom are prescribed in the context of making and *supplying* copies. In the context of *receiving* copies under ss. 41 and 42 [paras. 6.3.64 and 6.3.65], all the libraries comprised in Part A of Schedule 1 to the Regulations [para. 6.3.56] are again prescribed, but this time with the addition of all the libraries specified in Part B to that Schedule, namely non-profit making libraries outside the United Kingdom which are established to facilitate or encourage the study of bibliography, education, fine arts, history, languages, law, literature, medicine, music, philosophy, religion, science (including natural and social science) and technology.

6.3.58   In accordance with ss. 38 and 39 of the Act, a librarian, or any other person acting on his behalf, may make and supply a copy of an article in a periodical, or a copy of part of a literary, dramatic or musical work to a person, without infringing copyright, if he is satisfied that that person requires the copy for the purposes of private study or research, and that it will not be used for any other purpose. Furthermore, the librarian must obtain from the person a signed declaration to this effect, as a precondition to supplying the copy. Schedule 2 of the Regulations contains a suggested form of declaration, which it terms 'Form A', as follows:

DECLARATION: COPY OF ARTICLE OR PART OF PUBLISHED WORK

To:
     The Librarian of .... Library
     [Address of Library]

Please supply me with a copy of:
     *the article in the periodical, the particulars of which are [
                                                                                                          ]

     *the part of the published work, the particulars of which are [
                                                                                                          ]

required by me for the purposes of research or private study.

2.   I declare that –
    (a) I have not previously been supplied with a copy of the same material by you or any other librarian;
    (b) I will not use the copy except for research or private study and will not supply a copy of it to any other person; and
    (c) to the best of my knowledge no other person with whom I work or study has made or intends to make, at or about the same time as this request, a request for substantially the same material for substantially the same purpose.

3.   I understand that if the declaration is false in a material particular the copy supplied to me by you will be an infringing copy and that I shall be liable for infringement of copyright as if I had made the copy myself.

                                              †Signature ....

                                              Date ....

Name ....

Address ....

            ....

            ....

*Delete whichever is inappropriate.
†This must be the personal signature of the person making the request. A stamped or typewritten signature, or the signature of an agent, is NOT acceptable.

6.3.59   It will be noted that the person making the declaration must state that he has not received a copy of the same material from the librarian concerned, not from any other librarian, and also that, to the best of his belief, no other person with whom he studies or works has made or is about to make a similar request for similar material. It will also be noted that the footnotes to Form A specify that the declaration must be signed personally by the person requiring the copy, with stamped or typewritten signatures, and signatures by agents, being expressly prohibited.

6.3.60   Form A makes it clear that the librarian must be satisfied that the person is not acquiring a number of copies of the same material by applying for it from different sources. The librarian must also be satisfied that the person seeking the copy is not obtaining more than one copy of an article in a periodical, nor a copy of more than one article from any one issue of a periodical, nor a copy of more than a reasonable proportion of a published work. Neither the Regulations nor the Act give any indication as to what constitutes a 'reasonable proportion', and accordingly this will remain a question of fact to be determined in each case.

6.3.61   The Regulations deal not only with the problem of multiple copying by an individual, but also with the corresponding problem of multiple copying by different people acting in concert. The content of para. 2 (c) of Form A makes it clear that the person requesting the copy must satisfy a librarian on this score.

6.3.62   The Regulations provide that a librarian must charge the person requesting the copy the proper costs incurred in providing the copy, and that any sum which is charged must include a contribution towards the general expenses of the library.

6.3.63   In many cases it may be difficult to establish the exact purpose for which a person requires a copy, and a librarian will have little effective option other than to rely on the word of the person making the request. Because of this, the Regulations provide that once a librarian has received a signed declaration, he may rely on it to the extent that he may accept that the copies are required for private study or research. He may not, however, rely on it to satisfy himself of any of the other preconditions, nor, of course, may he rely on it if he knows it to be false. Thus a librarian enjoys only partial protection from any potential liability for aiding and abetting an infringement of the Act. However, turning to the other party to the transaction, any person who makes a declaration which is false in a material particular will himself be treated as if he had made the infringing copies and he could, therefore, be personally liable for the resulting infringement of the owner's copyright.

6.3.64   Turning from the provision of copies for research and private study, s. 41 and reg. 5 enable the librarian of a prescribed library to make certain copies and supply them to another prescribed library. This provision covers the copying of any article in a periodical, or the copying of the whole or part of a published edition, provided that the receiving libray does not receive more than one copy of each item, or, where multiple copies are provided, the receiving library states in writing that it is a prescribed library and that it does not know, and cannot by reasonable inquiry ascertain, the name and address of the person who is entitled to authorize the copying. The supplying applicant must pay a sum not less than the cost of the copying, including a contribution to the general expenses of the library.

6.3.65 Similarly, s. 42 and reg. 6, provide that librarians of prescribed libraries may, without infringing copyright, make copies of items in their permanent collections either for their own benefit by way of preserving or replacing the item, or for the benefit of the permanent collection of another prescribed library which has experienced damage to, or loss or destruction of, its own example of the item in question. Such copying is subject to certain conditions. Where the copying is for the benefit of the library which owns the item in question, it will be permitted only where the purchase of another example of the item would not be reasonably practicable. Where the copying is for the benefit of another library, that library must provide a written statement to the effect that its own example of the item has been lost, destroyed or damaged and that the purchase of another example is not reasonably practicable. The receiving library must also pay a sum not less than the cost of copying, including a contribution to the general expenses of the library.

6.3.66 Lastly, by virtue of s. 43 and reg. 7, the whole or part of *unpublished* works can be copied for the purpose of research or private study, without infringing copyright, as long as the student is allowed only one copy and he pays a sum not less than the cost of copying, including a contribution to the general expenses of the library. The applicant must also deliver to the librarian a signed declaration in substantially the same form as that contained in Schedule 2 to the Regulations under the title 'Form B', which is as follows:

DECLARATION: COPY OF WHOLE OR PART OF UNPUBLISHED WORK

To:
    The *Librarian/Archivist of .... *Library/Archive
    [Address of Library/Archive]

Please supply me with a copy of:
    the *whole/following part [particulars of part] of the [particulars of the unpublished work]
    required by me for the purposes of research or private study.

    2. I declare that –
        (a) I have not previously been supplied with a copy of the same material by you or any
            other librarian or archivist;
        (b) I will not use the copy except for research or private study and will not supply a copy of
            it to any other person; and
        (c) to the best of my knowledge the work had not been published before the document was
            deposited in your *library/archive and the copyright owner has not prohibited copying
            of the work.

    3. I understand that if the declaration is false in a material particular the copy supplied to me
by you will be an infringing copy and that I shall be liable for infringement of copyright as if I had
made the copy myself.

                          †Signature ....
                          Date ....

Name ....
Address ....
               ....
               ....

*Delete whichever is inappropriate.
†This must be the personal signature of the person making the request. A stamped or typewritten signature, or the
signature of an agent, is NOT acceptable.

6.3.67 As an examination of Form B shows, the applicant must declare
that he requires the copy for private study or research, has not received
a copy of the same material from elsewhere, will not supply a copy to
any other person and, to the best of his knowledge, the work is
unpublished and copying has not been forbidden by the copyright owner.
Again, not only does this declaration serve to protect the librarian in
the same way as the declaration contained in Form A, but also, as with
Form A, the maker of a false declaration is liable to the owner of the
copyright as if he had made the copy himself. For obvious reasons, this
exception does not apply if the copyright owner has expressly forbidden
copying of the work and the librarian making the copy is, or ought to
be, aware of that fact. In accordance with the general scheme of this
part of the legislation, the applicant must, of course, pay a sum not less
than the cost of copying, including a contribution to the general expenses

of the library.

6.3.68 The 1988 Act does not deal specifically with the problem of self-service photocopying machines whereby the user, under no guidance from the librarian, is able to copy whatever he wishes on payment of the requisite fee. Going back to first principles, it will be recalled that basically only the copyright owner has the right to copy his work, and that copying by anyone else is an infringement of the Act. Infringement also occurs if a person authorizes someone else to do any of the restricted acts. The key question is, therefore, what constitutes 'authorization'?

6.3.69 It can be argued that the provision of self-service copying facilities is impliedly an authorization, by the library authority or the librarian, for others to infringe copyright. This argument succeeded in the Australian test case of *Moorhouse and Angus and Robertson (Publishers) Pty Limited v. University of New South Wales* (1976), where the High Court of Australia decided that the University had authorized the photocopying of a work, even though the librarian did not know what was being copied. In the opinion of the court, the mere provision of the photocopier with no effective control over its use was enough to amount to authorization.

6.3.70 The Whitford Committee acknowledged this particular difficulty and recommended that a special licensing scheme be established to deal with self-service photocopying machines. The person responsible for the machine would be obliged to take out a licence and copies made on a licensed machine would not be treated as infringing copyright. Although, the 1988 Act did not specifically provide for this, the establishment of the Copyright Tribunal and the extensive provisions for licensing schemes would indicate that this suggestion could be put into effect.

6.3.71 It is, of course, common for self-service photocopiers to have notices fixed to, or positioned near, them warning people that the making of copies for anything other than the 'excepted acts' is an infringement of copyright. The Australian court in *Moorhouse* was not impressed by the notice affixed near to that machine because it did not explain the law clearly enough to the layman.

6.3.72 Although there appears to be no direct English authority, an interesting analogy can be drawn with the case of *C.B.S. Songs Ltd. and Others v. Amstrad Consumer Electronics plc and Another* (1988). The *Amstrad* case concerned the makers of twin decked, tape recording machines which had the facility of taping directly from one cassette onto another. The plaintiff alleged that this, together with the defendant's method of advertising the machines, encouraged home taping of copyright material, and that therefore the defendant was authorizing an infringement of copyright. The House of Lords rejected this argument, holding that there was no infringement by the defendant who had made it plain in its advertisements that it had no authority to grant the required permission.

Furthermore, the defendant had no control over the use of the machines which could be utilized for both legal and illegal purposes The mere fact that the tape machines could be used in breach of copyright did not amount to authorization to use them in that way. During the course of the judgement their Lordships considered the *Moorhouse* case [paras. 6.3.69 and 6.3.71], but pointed out that the major distinction between the two cases was the control over the equipment used. The library had some control over its photocopier, whereas Amstrad had no control over the tape-decks once they had been sold.

6.3.73 There are two obvious potential solutions to the uncertainty which exists in English law within the library context. The first is for the Copyright Tribunal to initiate an appropriate licensing scheme [para. 6.3.43]. Secondly, some prescribed form could be issued, the display of which would exculpate libraries and librarians. Until either of these happen, however, the best course of action would appear to be to display as clear a notice as possible, bearing in mind the inherent complexity and uncertainty of the law in this area.

PUBLIC LENDING RIGHT

6.4.01 The Public Lending Right system was created by the Public Lending Right Act 1979 and the Public Lending Right Scheme 1982 (Commencement) Order 1982, as subsequently amended. The scheme, with its consolidated amendments is available as Statutory Instrument 1988, No. 2070. The idea behind public lending right is simply that authors should be paid in respect of borrowings of their books from public libraries.

6.4.02 A basic point of distinction between copyright and public lending right is that the latter is still dependent on registration, whereas the former is not. The register is maintained by the Registrar of Public Lending Right, whose office is at Stockton-on-Tees.

6.4.03 To be eligible for registration for public lending right, a book must have an eligible author named on ts title page, and be printed and bound. For these purposes, the term 'author' includes writers, editors, compilers, illustrators and translators, and in order to be eligible an author must be resident in either the United Kingdom or the Federal Republic of Germany. The requirement that a book must be bound is satisfied by paperbacks as well as by cased editions. Additionally, the book must have been put on sale, and must not be a newspaper, magazine, journal or periodical nor must it be a musical score. Furthermore, it must not have more than three authors or illustrators named on the title page, and the authorship must be personal, rather than institutional. The last point means that, for example, an income tax guide written in the name of a firm of accountants would not qualify.

6.4.04   Different versions and editions of a book each count as separate books for public lending right purposes. For example, a two volume book, which is available in both hard and soft covers, will count as four books.

6.4.05   The allocation of payments to authors is based on a sampling system of all public library loans. Until 1989, the sample consisted of all the loans from 20 public libraries spread through England, Scotland, Wales and Northern Ireland. In 1989 the sample was increased to 30 libraries. The sample varies from time to time, with no library being eligible for inclusion for more than four years, and the practice being to drop at least 10 libraries a year, and replace them with others from the same region. The system is computerized and the computer is sufficiently sophisticated to detect abnormalities which would result from borrowers seeking to enhance an author's public lending right entitlement by a campaign of over-borrowing his books.

6.4.06   No author will be entitled to a public lending right payment if the sum involved would be less than £1.00 in any one year, and similarly there is an upper limit whereby no author can receive more than £6,000 in any one year. Although it will be obvious that many best-selling authors will benefit from the maximum payments, the Registrar of Public Lending Right has said that 'even among those authors who qualify for the maximum £6,000, about one third are relatively unknown'. Money which fails to be distributed through the application of these limits is returned to the fund, and thus become eligible for re-allocation to other authors.

6.4.07   The money which is used is quite distinct from that which is used to buy library books. Public lending right funds come from a Parliamentary allocation, in respect of which the Minister for the Arts has departmental responsibility. In 1988/89 the sum involved was £3,500,000.

6.4.08   Public lending right continues for 50 years after the author's death, and can be renounced or assigned by him during his lifetime, and it can pass on his death either by his will or on his intestacy. Public lending right is totally distinct from copyright, and there is therefore no objection to the two sets of rights being owned by different people.

6.4.09   The Registrar of Public Lending Right not only produces a range of helpful publicity material, but is also willing to give advice on the operation of the scheme in difficult cases.

7 The user's liability to the library

7.1.01 This chapter will consider the relationship between the library and the library user, with particular reference to the user's responsibility for library property which he has borrowed, and to his conduct whilst he is on library premises. This will necessitate referring back to the elements of the law of contract [paras. 2.6.01 *et seq*.], before looking at the special conditions of borrowing which library users accept, and some relevant aspects of the criminal law.

THE LEGAL NATURE OF THE RELATIONSHIP BETWEEN LIBRARIES AND LIBRARY USERS

7.2.01 At first sight, it seems obvious that there is a contract between the providers of library services and the users of those services. In the case of commercial libraries this first impression is no doubt accurate. However, in the case of the most common transaction, namely the borrowing of a book from a public library, the position is not so clear.

7.2.02 The difficulty stems from the fact that all contracts, except those made in the form of a deed, require consideration [para. 2.6.13], coupled with the fact that public library authorities have a duty to provide library services under s. 7 of the Public Libraries and Museums Act 1964 [para. 2.4.03 *et seq*.]. As a matter of the general law of contract, there is a measure of uncertainty as to whether the performance of a legal duty can amount to giving consideration. On the one hand there are cases such as *Stilk v. Myric* (1809), where two seamen deserted during the course of the voyage. The captain agreed to share the wages of the deserters between the remaining seamen if they completed the voyage to London. At the end of the voyage, the captain refused to pay the additional wages. The court held that the seamen, being under a legal obligation to sail the ship in any event, had provided no consideration and therefore were not legally entitled to the additional pay. This clearly

110

supports the general proposition that the doing of an act in performance of a legal duty cannot amount to consideration.

7.2.03 On the other hand, some commentators, notably *Chitty on Contracts* (25th edition, para. 183), argue that the law's refusal to enforce such promises is based on arguments that enforcement would be contrary to public policy, rather than on any absence of consideration. The public policy argument rests on the proposition that it would be conducive to extortion if enforcement was possible in respect of promises to pay people for doing what they are legally obliged to do anyway. This argument may seem less than realistic.

7.2.04 If, as seems preferable, the correct analysis is that performance of a legal duty cannot constitute consideration, it must follow that the arrangements between libraries and their borrowers are non-contractual in nature.

7.2.05 Fortunately, in purely practical terms, nothing turns on the way this particular problem is resolved, since the nature of the relationship between libraries and their borrowers is clearly that of *bailor* and *bailee*, with the books which are borrowed being the subject of a *bailment*. The question of whether or not the bailment is contractual appears to be of no practical relevance.

THE NATURE OF BAILMENT

7.3.01 A bailment is a transaction where possession of property is transferred from one person to another (respectively, the bailor and the bailee), subject to a condition, either express or implied, that the property will be returned to the bailor or dealt with in accordance with his instructions. Both elements of the transaction must be present. Thus, for example, when a library user leaves a pushchair or a shopping bag in part of a library designated for this purpose while choosing books, the library authority does not become a bailee because there has been no transfer of possession. Similarly, where there is a loan of cash there will be no bailment because although the loan is to be repaid, neither party expects the repayment to consist of exactly the same notes and coins which the lender transferred to the borrower.

7.3.02 There is a substantial body of law covering the obligations of each party to a bailment, but obviously, where the parties have expressly agreed terms, those terms will usually be of the first importance. In the context of libraries such express terms will be found in the regulations governing the conditions of borrowing, which the user will have accepted on joining the library.

The conditions of borrowing

7.3.03 Each library will have its own regulations specifying various conditions which its borrowers agree to accept, with some conditions imposing liability on the borrower and others imposing liability on the library authority. Typical conditions relate to such matters as the number of books which can be borrowed at any one time, the period of loan, the possibility of making reservations for books, the need to check out each book at the issue desk, and the imposition of fines when books are not returned in the prescribed time. Some of the conditions will overlap with the byelaws and even with the law of theft and criminal damage, for example conditions relating to conduct on the library premises; or with the general law, for example liability for loss or damage to a book could be both a breach of the conditions and also a criminal offence [paras. 7.4.01 *et seq*.].

7.3.04 The fact that the parties have agreed terms does not necessarily mean that the court will simply enforce those terms. For example, in para. 2.6.06 a case was discussed where the court considered the word 'lucky' to be so vague as to be incapable of creating an enforceable claim. Furthermore, at an even earlier stage in the process of judicial decision-making, the court will have had to conclude that the parties actually did agree the term in question, and the more onerous the term is, the greater is the degree of persuasion which the court will require. The case of *Interfoto Picture Library Ltd. v. Stiletto Visual Programmes Ltd.* (1988) is instructive.

7.3.05 The facts were that the defendant borrowed 47 transparencies from the plaintiff's photographic lending library. The transparencies duly arrived at the defendant's premises with a delivery note. The delivery note clearly stated that the transparencies were to be returned to the library by 19 March and, under the prominent heading *CONDITIONS*, the note also contained nine conditions. One of these stated that the sum of £5 per day, plus VAT, would be charged as a 'holding fee' in respect of each transparency not returned by the due date. Unfortunately, the defendant forgot about the transparencies and did not return them until 2 April. As a result the plaintiff sent to the defendant an invoice for a 'holding fee' amounting to £3783.50. Perhaps not surprisingly, the defendant refused to pay, with the result that the plaintiff brought an action to recover the money.

7.3.06 At the trial the judge found for the plaintiff, deciding that the conditions were prominently displayed and formed part of the contract between the parties. The Court of Appeal, however, reversed the decision, on the basis that where it is alleged that a contract contains a clause which is particularly onerous or unusual, and the clause would not generally be known to the other party, the party seeking to enforce the clause had to show that the clause had been brought to the attention of that party. The Court of Appeal then found that the clause in question was unreasonable and extortionate, and therefore that it did not form part of the contract because it had not been sufficiently clearly brought to the defendant's attention. However, even though the appeal was allowed, the court ordered the defendant to pay £3.50 per week for each overdue transparency, on the basis that this sum was fair in all the circumstances.

7.3.07   The fact that the *Interfoto* case involved a commercially operated library is a clear point of distinction between it and the public library service, where, as we have seen, there will probably not be a contractual relationship between the library and the user. Nevertheless, the case serves as a useful reminder that if reliance is placed on the conditions of borrowing as the basis of the terms of the bailment, the court may need to be persuaded that these were effectively communicated to the user, and that the conditions are reasonable in themselves. The requirement of effective communication may mean, for example, the provision of copies in large print, or multi-lingual form.

CRIMINAL LIABILITY

7.4.01   There are various headings under which a library user may be criminally liable in relation to his use of the library and its property. These will be discussed by reference to library byelaws, the somewhat specialized Library Offences Act 1898, the Public Health (Control of Diseases) Act 1984, the Theft Act 1968, the Criminal Damage Act 1971, and the Criminal Law Act 1977. Finally, the problem of dealing with badly behaved children will be discussed.

Library byelaws

7.4.02   In common with many other public and semi-public bodies such as nationalized undertakings like British Rail, local authorities have statutory powers to make byelaws. Etymologically, the 'bye' element of the word 'byelaw' is the same as the 'by' ending which is common in English place-names, such as Whitby. This explains the original nature of byelaws, which were laws of local application, in the sense that they applied only within the particular town in respect of which they were made. This remains the essence of byelaws, although obviously in the case of, for example, British Rail, the restriction on the area of a byelaw's operation will be determined by reference to the extent of the authority's property, rather than to a single locality. It is in the nature of a byelaw that it:

> necessarily involves restriction of liberty of action by persons who come under its operation as to acts which, but for the byelaw, they would be free to do or not to do as they pleased (*per* Lord Russell C.J. in *Kruse v. Johnson* (1898)).

7.4.03 Byelaws can be made under a number of specific statutes. Local authorities have a general power under s. 235 of the Local Government Act 1972, to make byelaws for 'the good rule and government' of their areas, dealing with matters as diverse as fouling of footpaths by dogs, and loitering at church doors. More specifically, section 19 of the Public Libraries and Museums Act 1964 gives library authorities power to make byelaws relating to libraries.

7.4.04 All byelaws are subject to confirmation by an appropriate Secretary of State, and there is a common practice for each Secretary of State to issue model byelaws, so that authorities wishing to make byelaws can be reasonably confident of the kind of byelaw which is likely to be confirmed. The adoption of provisions contained in model byelaws is not, however, compulsory, although in most cases it will be convenient. In the public library context, the Home Secretary has issued model byelaws, regulating the conduct of people on library premises as well as imposing various obligations in connection with the loan of library books. While each library authority will have its own byelaws which will vary in detail, it is useful to look generally at some typical provisions contained in model byelaws for libraries.

7.4.05 Under the model byelaws, a library officer (which simply means the Chief Librarian or anyone else employed for the purposes of the 1964 Act), is empowered to refuse admission to persons who are 'offensively unclean' (model byelaw no. 4). Other prohibitions include spitting on the premises (model byelaw no. 14), lying on the floor (model byelaw no. 20), and annoying other users in their proper use of the library (model byelaw no. 17). The model byelaws further prohibit careless or negligent damage to books (model byelaw no. 8), and failure to return books to the library within 14 days of being required to do so (model byelaw no. 12). A library officer has power to exclude or remove people who are contravening the byelaws if the offender's name and address are unknown and cannot be readily ascertained, or if the circumstances are such that the offender's continued presence may result in further contravention of the byelaws or in prejudice to the proper use and regulation of the library (model byelaw no. 25). At a practical level, of course, commonsense suggests that it would often be sensible to delay any confrontation until a police officer is present. The byelaws are enforced by means of prosecution in the magistrates' court, where convicted users may be fined.

7.4.06 A valid byelaw has the same force as any other enactment, but because byelaws are delegated legislation, the courts can inquire into whether or not they are valid, and can declare them to be void if they are ultra vires. This is, of course, in stark contradistinction to the position in relation to statutes, where the doctrine of the legislative supremacy of Parliament [para. 2.2.03] means that the courts have no choice but to implement any Act which is passed.

7.4.07   There are four tests for the validity of byelaws. Obviously, there should be no difficulty in practice with any of these tests if the model byelaws are adopted, but if anything more original is attempted, the tests for validity must be taken into account. It is also interesting to note that it has been held that if a byelaw is void, the fact that it has been confirmed by the appropriate Secretary of State does not validate it (*R. v. Wood* (1885)).

7.4.08   The first test, which merely reflects the basic doctrine of *ultra vires*, is that the byelaw must be within the powers of the body which makes it. The courts are likely to construe this test strictly in the case of a byelaw which imposes criminal liability, as virtually all byelaws do. For example, the court quashed a conviction under a byelaw requiring occupiers of premises to remove snow from the footpath outside their premises, because the relevant statute listed only 'dust, ashes, rubbish, filth, manure, dung and soil' as the materials whose removal could be required (*R. v. Wood* (1885)). Secondly and thirdly, the case of *Kruse v. Johnson* (1898), established that a byelaw must be reasonable in the *Wednesbury* sense of that word [para. 2.3.17], and its terms must be sufficiently certain to enable people to know what they must do, or not do, in order to comply with it. Fourthly, a byelaw must neither permit something which a statute prohibits, nor prohibit something which a statute permits (*Powell v. May* (1946)).

The Libraries Offences Act 1898

7.4.09   The Libraries Offences Act 1898 applies only to libraries and reading rooms maintained by registered Industrial and Provident Societies, Friendly Societies, and Trades' Unions (s. 3(b) of the Act). These bodies have no byelaw-making powers, and the effect of the Act is to create some of the offences which would typically be found in a public library authority's byelaws.

7.4.10   Where the Act applies, it is an offence to annoy or disturb other users by behaving in a disorderly manner, using violent, abusive or obscene language, betting or gambling, and persisting in remaining on the premises beyond the hours fixed for closing, having first been given proper warning.

The Public Health (Control of Diseases) Act 1984

7.4.11   It is an offence for a person suffering from a 'notifiable disease' to borrow, or cause to be borrowed on their behalf, any book from a public library. Similarly, any person who has in their possession a library book and later discovers that they are suffering from such a disease is obliged to report the fact to the library authority (s. 25 of the Public Health (Control of Diseases) Act 1984). The authority then becomes under a duty to cause the book to be disinfected or destroyed.

7.4.12   Section 10 of the Act provides that 'notifiable disease' means cholera, plague, relapsing fever, smallpox and typhus, whilst s. 16 gives local authorities power to specify other diseases as being notifiable, subject to the approval of the Secretary of State. Additionally, a series of Regulations have been issued under which the following are also notifiable dieases: rabies, lassa fever, viral haemorrhagic fever and marburg disease.

Theft

7.4.13   The Theft Act 1968 provides that a person is guilty of theft if he:

dishonestly appropriates property belonging to another with the intention of permanently depriving the other of it (s. 1).

In addition to the obvious type of situation, a person can also be guilty of theft if he originally acquires the property legitimately, but subsequently forms a dishonest intention to deprive the owner of the property, and actually does so (s. 3(1) of the 1968 Act). In many disputed cases, the argument centres on whether there was actually a dishonest intention on the part of the defendant. Depending on all the circumstances of the case, this could amount to an assertion by him that he thought he was entitled to keep the property, or, more usually, in the shoplifting type of case, it will amount to an assertion by the defendant that he was absent-minded rather than dishonest. Where a defence of absent-mindedness is raised, as it could well be in the case of the illegitimate removal of a book from a library, the onus is on the prosecution to prove beyond reasonable doubt that in fact the defendant was dishonest. This can be very difficult to do, and together with the fact that any defendant charged with any theft is entitled to be tried by a jury at the Crown Court, this difficulty may explain why there are very few prosecutions for theft of library books, compared with the number of prosecutions under the byelaws, where no dishonesty need be established and where the cases must be tried by the magistrates' court.

Criminal damage

7.4.14   The Criminal Damage Act 1971 provides that it is an offence for a person without lawful excuse to destroy or damage any property belonging to another, if he *intends* to destroy or damage the property or if he is *reckless* as to whether the property would be destroyed or damaged. Clearly, in common with theft, this offence can be committed in relation to library books, although in the case of criminal damage there is no right of trial by jury unless the value of the property exceeds £2,000. The state of mind which the law characterizes as *recklessness* is less precise than *intention*.

7.5.15   The leading House of Lords case which defines recklessness as part of its *ratio decidendi* is *R. v. Lawrence* (1971), where Lord Diplock, with the agreement of the other Law Lords, said:

> Recklessness on the part of the doer of an act presupposes that there is something in the circumstances that would have drawn the attention of an ordinary prudent individual to the possibility that his act was capable of causing the kind of serious harmful consequences that the section which created the offence was intended to prevent, and that the risk of those harmful consequences occurring was not so slight that an ordinary prudent individual would feel justified in treating them as negligible. It is only when this is so that the doer of the act is acting 'recklessly' if, before doing the act, he either fails to give any thought to the possibility of there being no such risk or, having recognised that there was such a risk, he nevertheless goes on to do it.

7.4.16   For example, the court might conclude that an ordinary prudent individual would perceive that leaving a library book unattended on a beach while the tide is coming in would come within the *Lawrence* test, if, in the event, the book becomes waterlogged.

7.4.17   Perhaps the most celebrated offences of theft and damage in relation to library books were those committed by Joe Orton and Kenneth Halliwell, for which Old Street Magistrates' Court in London sentenced them each to six months' imprisonment. Modern views on sentencing policy mean that such a heavy sentence would be very unlikely now, even bearing in mind the relatively substantial value of the books concerned, namely approximately £450 (at 1962 prices).

Criminal Law Act 1977

7.4.18   In addition to the power of library employees to exclude or remove people from library premises where an appropriate byelaw is in force [para. 7.4.05], it is worth noticing that s. 6 of the Criminal Law Act 1977 makes it an offence for any person to try to gain entry to any premises, without permission, by using or threatening to use violence. The violence mentioned in the Act does not need to be directed at a person refusing entry, and therefore the offence could be committed by directing the violence, or the threat of violence, at the property in question. Thus, for example, a person who has previously been excluded or removed from a library may well be refused entry in future. If, in an attempt to get in, that person threatens to damage library property, he could be committing an offence under s. 6 of the 1977 Act. This offence is triable only by the Magistrates' Court.

Control of children

7.4.19 Certain people, such as school-teachers, are said to be *in loco parentis*. Broadly speaking, this means that they have the same immediate rights to control a child as the child's own parent would have. However, a librarian would not come into this category, and therefore the question arises as to the extent of a librarian's lawful power to control children. Unfortunately, this is a somewhat grey area of law.

7.4.20 The prime risk which a librarian runs if he lays hands on a child is that he may render himself liable to be sued, or even to be prosecuted, for assault. One provision which may be of use is s. 3 of the Criminal Law Act 1967. This provides that anyone may use such force as is reasonable in the circumstances in the prevention of crime, or in detaining an offender. Obviously, the question of what is reasonable in the circumstances is the crucial consideration, and in relatively trivial offences (judged against the whole range of possible criminality), only a relatively small amount of force will be justifiable. Moreover, a further difficulty arises in relation to children.

7.4.21 There is an irrebuttable presumption that a child under the age of 10 cannot commit a criminal offence (s. 50, Children and Young Persons Act 1933, as amended by s. 16, Children and Young Persons Act 1963). In relation to children over the age of 10 but under the age of 14, there is a similar presumption at Common Law, except that this presumption is rebuttable by evidence.

7.4.22 It follows, therefore, that s. 3 of the Criminal Law Act 1967 can never be relied upon to justify the use of force against children under the age of 10. In the case of 10 to 14 year olds, if the prosecution is to rebut the presumption, it must show that the child knew that what he was doing was seriously wrong. It is not necessary to show that the child knew that what he was doing was morally wrong, but on the other hand it is insufficient to show merely that the child knew that what he was doing was naughty or mischievous.

7.4.23 It follows from this that although a child aged between 10 and 14 appears to be committing an offence, the court may conclude that what he was doing was not actually an offence, because the prosecution has failed to rebut the presumption. It also follows that in such circumstances anyone who, relying on s. 3 of the 1967 Act, seeks to justify the use of force against the child, may find himself in a very exposed position. The safest course, when faced with apparently criminal conduct on the part of the young, is to call the police and let them worry about the consequences.

8 The library's liability to the user

8.1.01 The main focus of this chapter will be those aspects of the law of tort which are relevant to anyone who occupies premises. More specifically, it will consider the circumstances in which members of the public (and, for that matter, employees as well) may be able to bring claims in respect of loss, damage or injury suffered by them whilst they are on local authority premises. The areas of law which are principally relevant are *occupiers' liability* and *negligence*. Additionally, although it is not connected with the occupation of premises, it will convenient when discussing negligence to mention the problem of the possibility of liability arising from the giving of bad advice, or negligent misstatement to be more technical.

8.1.02 Although for convenience of explanation these two areas of law are dealt with separately, it is important to remember that in practice they are far from being self-contained, both of them being areas of law which overlap, so that one fact situation may well give rise to both types of liability.

OCCUPIERS' LIABILITY

8.2.01 The Occupiers' Liability Act 1957 imposes on occupiers of premises a *common duty of care* which is owed to all *visitors*, which in this context means anyone who is *lawfully* on the premises. (Trespassers, who are of course present *unlawfully*, are considered in paras. 8.2.16– 20.) The Act defines the key word *premises* very widely, to include 'any fixed or movable structure'. The courts have held that ladders and scaffolding are 'movable structures' within the terms of the Act.

Who is an *occupier*?

8.2.02 Although the Act does not define the word 'occupier', it is nevertheless clear that for someone to be an occupier he must have a measure of control over the premises. An owner who has relinquished all control, perhaps to a tenant, is no longer an 'occupier'. In contrast, a person temporarily in control of premises, but without complete possession, could be an occupier within the terms of the Act. Similarly, if two or more persons share control, there could be more than one occupier at any one time.

8.2.03   By way of illustration, consider the position when a workman arrives on local authority premises in order to repair the roof tiles which have become dislodged in a gale. To reach the roof, he uses a ladder belonging to the local authority. The ladder is, of course, 'premises' within the definition of the Act. While the workman is using the ladder it is under his control and therefore he is responsible for it. However, if a member of the local authority staff held the ladder while the workman was carrying out his task, complete control would not have been transferred. In those circumstances, there could be two 'occupiers' for the purposes of the Act.

8.2.04   In the case of *Wheat v. E. Lacon & Co. Ltd.* (1966), there is a lengthy discussion centring on this point. The facts were that a brewery owned a public house, the first floor of which was used by the brewery's manager as living accommodation. The brewery allowed the manager to take in paying guests for his own profit. One of these guests fell down the stairs in the private portion of the premises and was killed. The court held that in this situation both the brewery and the manager were occupiers. The brewery retained control of the premises to the extent that they were responsible for structural repairs to the property, but the manager was in control on a day to day basis.

8.2.05   Although this case gives guidance in ascertaining who could be the occupier, it is not exhaustive and the courts have repeatedly held that every situation will be decided on its own particular facts, taking into account the nature of the occupation, the degree of physical possession of the premises and the extent of the control exercised over it.

Who is a *visitor?*

8.2.06   Who, then, is a visitor? Anyone who is invited, either expressly or by implication, on to the premises will be there lawfully, as will any person (such as a gas board official or policeman) who enters as of right. However, the occupier's duty will extend only to those parts of the premises to which the visitor is invited. As Scrutton L.J. said in *The Calgarth* (1927):

> When you invite a person into your house to use the stairs you do not invite him to slide down the bannisters.

The common duty of care

8.2.07 The 'common duty of care' is described in s. 2 of the Act:

(1) An occupier of premises owes the same duty the 'common duty of care', to all his visitors except in so far as he is free to and does extend, restrict, modify, or exclude his duty to any visitor or visitors by agreement or otherwise.

(2) The 'common duty of care' is a duty to take such care as, in all the circumstances of the case is reasonable to see that a visitor will be reasonably safe in using the premises for the purposes for which he is invited or permitted by the occupier to be there.

8.2.08 Again, every case will turn on its own individual facts, but in endeavouring to establish the extent of the duty, the court will have regard to a variety of factors, including the size of the risk, the likelihood of injury and the cost of avoiding it.

8.2.09 Section 2(3) also specifies that 'an occupier must be prepared for children to be less careful than adults' and, further, that he 'is entitled to expect that a person exercising his calling will appreciate and guard against special risks ordinarily incidental to it'. As an example of the latter, two chimney sweeps were killed when they inhaled carbon monoxide fumes whilst sealing up a ventilation shaft on the defendant's premises. The sweeps were aware of the presence of the fumes; therefore the court held that this was a special risk ordinarily incidental to the plaintiffs' line of work and accordingly the occupier owed no duty to them in respect of it (*Roles v. Nathan* (1963)).

8.2.10 On the other hand, when children are lawful visitors, the law expects additional care to be taken by an occupier on their behalf. By their very nature, children are more susceptible to risk, not only from inherent dangers, but also from their natural inquisitiveness, which may tempt them into situations which an adult would avoid. Thus, a local authority has been held liable when a child died as a result of eating brightly coloured, poisonous berries in a public park (*Glasgow Corporation v. Taylor* (1921)). Perhaps more obviously, in *Moloney v. Lambeth London Borough Council* (1966), an occupier was found liable when a four year-old boy fell through the bars of a balustrade. The gaps between the bars were such that any small child could have fallen through; thus the condition of the staircase, with its obvious danger to young children, indicated that the occupier had not fulfilled his duty of care.

8.2.11 However, an occupier will not always be liable for children's accidents, particularly if he could reasonably have assumed that the child would be accompanied by an adult or an older child. In *Phipps v. Rochester Corporation* (1955) a five year-old fell into a trench on a building site. The occupiers were held not liable because, in the words of Devlin J:

> ... the responsibility for the safety of little children must rest primarily on the parents; it is their duty to see that such children are not allowed to wander about by themselves ... it would not be socially desirable if parents were, as a matter of course, able to shift the burden of looking after their children off their own shoulders.

However, the judge did conclude that different considerations might apply to public places, where parents might expect their children to be reasonably safe. Clearly a public library could be such a place.

Defences

8.2.12 This 'common duty of care' which is imposed on the occupier by the Act would appear to be very far-reaching. However, its effects are curtailed by the availability to the occupier of a number of defences. First, a visitor may voluntarily accept a risk, thus shouldering the responsibility himself. Secondly, he may contribute to his injuries by his own negligence and thus relieve the occupier of part of his burden. The Act also expressly provides that an occupier may warn a visitor of a risk and, as long as the warning was adequate in the circumstances, this will discharge the occupier's liability. However, in order to provide effective protection, such a warning notice must be of adequate size and be prominently positioned. In multi-racial areas an occupier should also consider the possibility of translating his notice into those foreign languages which are commonly encountered in the locality. What is reasonable will always depend on the particular circumstances of each case, but a prudent occupier should think carefully about the steps needed to give adequate forewarning to visitors.

8.2.13 Further, under s. 2 (1), where the occupier has a contract with the visitor, there may be a disclaimer clause in the contract. Alternatively, the occupier may display a notice saying that persons entering do so at their own risk. A visitor would then be accepting the occupier's terms when he set foot on the premises. It is important to note, however, that any attempt to exclude liability in either of these ways must comply with the terms of the Unfair Contract Terms Act 1977. This Act prohibits the restriction of liability for death or personal injury resulting from negligence which arises from the occupation of premises for business purposes. 'Business purposes' includes the use of premises for the purposes of a local authority.

8.2.14 Lastly, an occupier will not be liable for faulty work carried out by an independent contractor employed by him, for example, to repair the staircase, if it is reasonable for the occupier to rely on the competence of the contractor. Before an occupier can take advantage of this provision of the Act, he must have taken all reasonable steps to ensure that the work was done correctly. It would not be possible to escape liability if the occupier could have discovered for himself by careful inspection that the staircase had been repaired with, for example, rotten timber. In the case of *Ferguson v. Welsh and Others* (1987) the House of Lords had to consider this section of the Act. The facts, briefly, were that a local authority invited tenders to demolish a number of buildings on a site owned by it. The tender of one company was accepted and the company employed two brothers to carry out the work. One of the brothers invited the plaintiff to help them without notifying the local authority of the invitation. During the course of the demolition work, which was carried out in a dangerous manner, the plaintiff was seriously injured. He sued the local authority, as well as the contractor, on the basis that the council was liable in its capacity as one of the occupiers of the premises. The House of Lords, however, found for the local authority. Their Lordships held that a person who engages an independent contractor, as long as they are satisfied as to the competence of that contractor, can take advantage of the provisions of the Act and rely on the skills of the contractor. Furthermore, in this instance, their Lordships were not satisfied that the plaintiff was a visitor within the meaning of the Act.

Personal property

8.2.15   The 1957 Act protects not only people who visit premises, but also any property which they bring with them (s. 1(3)).

The trespasser

8.2.16   The 1957 Act did not apply to people who were not lawful visitors, and therefore trespassers were excluded from its provisions. Until 1984, any trespassers who were injured had to rely on the very limited rights which the common law gave them.

8.2.17   The leading common law case of *British Railways Board v. Herrington* (1972) decided that although an occupier owed a duty of care to a trespasser, the extent of the duty was less than that which was owed to a lawful visitor. More specifically, as far as trespassers were concerned, the common duty of care was superseded by a duty to act in accordance with common humanity. The facts in *Herrington* concerned a young child who had climbed onto a railway line at a point where people were known to take a short cut across the line. British Rail had taken no steps to prevent the trespass and, when the boy was injured on the 'live' rail, they were held responsible.

8.2.18   The test established in *Herrington* was a subjective one, namely what steps would it be reasonable to expect *this* occupier to take in *these* circumstances? In an attempt to clarify the law and as a direct if somewhat belated result of this case, Parliament passed the Occupiers' Liability Act 1984. This Act deals expressly with the difficulties relating to persons who are not 'visitors' for the purposes of the 1957 Act, and who are, for the main part, trespassers.

8.2.19   The Act provides that an occupier is under a duty to a non-visitor when three factors are present. The occupier must not only be aware of the existence of a danger or potential danger on his premises, but must also know or have reasonable grounds to believe that trespassers will come into the vicinity of the danger, and it must also be reasonable to expect him to take some precautions against the risk in order to protect the trespasser.

8.2.20   It is inconceivable that an occupier could have a heavier burden in respect of unlawful visitors to his premises, so the Act enables him to discharge his duty by giving appropriate warnings, usually by way of displaying notices on his premises.

NEGLIGENCE

8.3.01   Leaving aside occupier's liability, the other major relevant area of the law of tort is negligence.

The elements of negligence

8.3.02   A plaintiff must prove three things to be successful in a negligence action. First, that the defendant owed the plaintiff a duty of care. Secondly, that the defendant breached that duty. Thirdly, that the damage suffered by the plaintiff resulted from the breach of the duty. Unless he can prove all three elements a plaintiff will not succeed. It is necessary, therefore, to look at these elements in more detail.

The duty of care

8.3.03   The decision of the House of Lords in *Donoghue v. Stevenson* (1932) established what has now become the classic test to determine when a duty of care arises. The plaintiff claimed that she suffered illness and shock as a result of drinking a bottle of ginger beer in which she found the remains of a decomposed snail. The House of Lords held that the manufacturer of ginger beer owed a duty of care to the plaintiff, even though there was no contractual relationship between the parties. At the level of principle, Lord Atkin attempted to define the circumstances from which the duty of care could spring:

> The rule that you are to love your neighbour becomes, in law, you must not injure your neighbour; and the lawyer's question who is my neighbour? receives a restricted reply. You must take reasonable care

to avoid acts or omissions which you can reasonably foresee would be likely to injure your neighbour. Who, then, in law is my neighbour? The answer seems to be — persons who are so closely and directly affected by my act that I ought reasonably to have them in contemplation as being so affected when I am directing my mind to the acts or omissions which are called in question.

8.3.04 Since this case, the law of negligence has developed. As a general rule it is necessary for a plaintiff to establish that there is sufficient proximity (or neighbourhood) between him and the defendant to justify the conclusion that the defendant owes him a duty of care.

Breach of the duty of care

8.3.05 Having established that the duty of care exists, the plaintiff must then prove that the defendant was in breach of that duty. To do this it is necessary to ascertain the standard of care to be expected. It will be recalled that Lord Atkin's test involves the concept of reasonableness, or, in other words, that the standard of care is the standard which can be expected of the 'reasonable man'.

8.3.06 Who is the 'reasonable man'? One classic statement is that he is the 'man on the Clapham omnibus'. Whatever phrase is used to describe the reasonable man, the essential point is that basically an objective standard is being used to gauge the way in which *this* defendant actually behaved as against the way in which a reasonable man would have behaved in the same situation.

8.3.07 In some circumstances, however, the objectivity of the reasonable man test can be softened by giving the reasonable man some of the attributes of the defendant. For example, a jeweller who pierced the ears of a customer was compared to a *reasonable jeweller* when ascertaining the standard of care which he should have attained. He was not expected to act as a *reasonable doctor* engaged in the same task (*Philips v. Whiteley (William) Ltd.* (1938)). Similarly, the standard of care expected from children would vary according to the child's age — a 13 year-old girl would thus be assumed to possess the knowledge of the reasonable 13 year-old. She would be expected to know that if she put her hand into the fire she would be likely to get her fingers burned. In contrast, a three year-old would not be expected to have such knowledge.

8.3.08 In assessing the appropriate standard of care it is possible to obtain guidance by looking at four factors — the likelihood of injury resulting from the defendant's act; the seriousness of that injury; the usefulness of the defendant's act; and the reasonableness of taking precautions to prevent the injury.

8.3.09 In *Bolton v. Stone* (1951) the plaintiff was hit by a cricket ball from a nearby cricket ground as she was walking along a public highway. However, as a cricket ball had only been hit out of the ground six times in 35 years, it was held that the likelihood of injury was so slight that the defendants were not in breach of their duty of care.

8.3.10   The seriousness of the injury was considered in the case of *Paris v. Stepney Borough Council* (1951), where a one-eyed welder was hit in his good eye by a splinter of metal. The council were held to be in breach of their duty of care because they had not provided the plaintiff with goggles (goggles were not generally provided at this time). The seriousness of the injury to the plaintiff was greater than it would have been to a two-eyed welder and the burden was also, therefore, greater.

8.3.11   In rare cases the usefulness of the defendant's act excuses the careless method of carrying out the act. In *Watt v. Hertfordshire County Council* (1954), a heavy jack on a fire engine slipped and injured a fireman when an emergency call was being answered. The importance of getting to the scene of an accident absolved the fire authority.

8.3.12   The importance of taking reasonable precautions may be illustrated by comparing two similar, yet vitally different, cases. First, in *Hopkins v. Scunthorpe Corporation* (1966), a child was injured as a result of slipping in the entrance hall of a public library. The accident occurred in the February of the long, cold winter of 1962−3. The plaintiff slipped in a pool of water on the floor of the library, just inside the entrance hall, but beyond a rubber mat which had been placed by the door. The water had accumulated on the floor from the melting snow which had been tramped in from the street. No additional precautions were taken by the library staff to mop up the water or lay additional mats and the court held the local authority liable for the child's injuries. The judge stated that, by February, it was reasonably foreseeable that snow would be 'walked' in and would melt on the library floor. In those circumstances it would have been reasonable for the defendant to take further action, at negligible cost, to prevent the occurrence of such accidents.

8.3.13   By way of contrast, in *Latimer v. A.E.C. Ltd.* (1953), the floor of the defendant's premises became wet during a thunderstorm. The defendant arranged for the floor to be covered in sawdust, but the plaintiff still slipped and injured himself. It was held, that in all the circumstances the defendant was not liable because he had taken all reasonable precautions.

8.3.14   The examples discussed in the previous paragraphs show that the standard of care to be achieved falls short of perfection. Nevertheless, an individual will be held liable for his own carelessness which he could reasonably have guarded against.

126

8.3.15 The third element in establishing a claim for negligence is that the plaintiff must show that he suffered injury or damage as a direct result of the defendant's breach of duty. This topic, which is known as causation, has two elements. First, there is causation in fact. This is neatly illustrated by the case of *Wakelin v. London and S.W. Railway Co.* (1886). The House of Lords were asked to find that the plaintiff's late husband had been killed as a result of the negligence of the railway company. Lord Halsbury L.C. said:

> One may surmise ... that the unfortunate man was knocked down by a passing train while on the level crossing; but assuming in the plaintiff's favour that fact to be established, is there anything to show that the train ran over the man, rather than the man ran against the train?

8.3.16 However, even if the plaintiff can prove that his injury was caused by the defendant's breach of duty, he must still persuade the court that the defendant should be made liable for the loss. This is the second aspect of causation, which is known as either causation in law or remoteness.

8.3.17 The basic test for remoteness was laid down in the case of *The Wagon Mound* (1961). The facts of the case are complex, but the essential point is that oil was discharged from a ship as a result of which there was a fire. The court held that the defendant should be liable for those consequences of his carelessness which a reasonable man would have foreseen. Thus, the defendant should have reasonably foreseen that the careless discharge of oil from its ship could have injured the plaintiff's premises, possibly by causing pollution. What could not have reasonably been foreseen was that the premises would burn down in a fire caused by the discharge of the oil. The defendant was, therefore, not liable for the fire damage to the plaintiff's premises.

8.3.18 Over the years a wide interpretation has been given to the idea of remoteness. In particular, a defendant will be liable even though he could not reasonably foresee the precise results of his negligence. This is particularly so where the extent of the damage is far greater than the defendant could have predicted. In *Bradford v. Robinson Rentals Ltd.* (1967), the plaintiff was a van driver who was exposed to extreme cold during the course of his driving duties and who suffered frost bite as a result. The defendants, who were his employers could not have reasonably foreseen that particular harm, but they could have reasonably foreseen some harm, such as influenza or pneumonia. Therefore, they were liable for the whole of the injury. Similarly, in *Ogwo v. Taylor* (1987), the defendant, who had negligently started a fire in his attic while burning off paint with a blowlamp, was held to be liable to a fireman who was seriously injured while fighting the blaze. The fireman's actual injuries resulted from scalding steam which the defendant could not have reasonably foreseen. However, the defendant could have reasonably foreseen that firemen would be called to the blaze and that they could suffer some injury as a result. Therefore, the House of Lords said, the defendant was liable.

Contributory negligence

8.3.19   Having looked at the steps which a plaintiff must take to prove his case in negligence, it is now necessary to consider the situation where the plaintiff is partly responsible for his own injuries – or, in other words, where the plaintiff is contributorily negligent. The answer lies in the Law Reform (Contributory Negligence) Act 1945, which provides that a plaintiff who is partially at fault shall have any compensation reduced to reflect his share in the responsibility. For example, in the majority of cases, a passenger who is injured in a car crash would be contributorily negligent if he was not wearing a seat belt, and therefore his damages would be reduced.

Negligent misstatement

8.3.20   For many years the courts held that there was no liability in negligence for a carelessly made statement, as opposed to a careless act. However, in 1963, in the leading case of *Hedley Byrne & Co. Ltd. v. Heller & Partners Ltd.*, the House of Lords indicated that a duty of care could arise when one person makes a statement to another on which he knows, or could reasonably expect, that other to rely. Lord Morris of Borth-y-Guest said:

> I consider ... that if someone possessed of a special skill undertakes to apply that skill for the assistance of another who relies on such skill, a duty of care will arise ... Furthermore, if ... a person takes it on himself to give information or advice to be passed on to another person who, as he knows or should know, will place reliance on it, then a duty of care will arise.

8.3.21   Since this case, liability has been extended through case law to virtually all professional people, including architects, engineers, solicitors and local government officers. Although, to date, liability has been restricted to advice given in a business context, it is possible that it could be extended to cover social occasions in the future. One of the crucial elements giving rise to the duty of care is the knowledge on the part of the defendant that another person will be relying on his skill and judgement. This could surely occur as much at the golf club as at the office.

8.3.22 The possibility of liability for negligent misstatement must clearly be of concern to librarians when they are performing their general advice-giving function. Obviously there is a tendency to want to be as helpful as possible. In practice there is no need to be unduly anxious, since by parallel reasoning the principle enunciated earlier in *Philips v. Whiteley (William) Ltd.* (1938) [para. 8.3.09] would no doubt apply in order to avoid the conclusion that a librarian was necessarily expert in all subjects. Nevertheless, it is important that a librarian, in common with everyone else, should not hold himself out as having more expertise than he actually has.

Omissions to Act

8.3.23 Since a duty is owed, in Lord Atkin's words, 'not to injure your neighbour,' [para. 8.3.03], does it follow that there is a corresponding duty in relation to omissions to act? Generally speaking, the answer is that there is not. There is no duty, for example, to dive into a lake and save a drowning child, although there are instances when a failure to act could give rise to a breach of the duty of care. Normally this would be when a special relationship exists between the parties, for example doctor and patient or teacher and pupil.

8.3.24 Also, some bodies, like local authorities, are under a duty imposed by statute to do various things. A local authority which fails to fulfil that duty could be sued for negligence if the plaintiff suffered damage as a result. An example of such a duty arises from the legislation currently contained in the Building Act 1984, under which a local authority is obliged to ensure compliance with the building regulations and is given a power to inspect buildings in the course of construction. It was held in *Anns v. London Borough of Merton* (1977), that failure to carry out that duty or failure to exercise proper discretion could amount to negligence.

Vicarious liability

8.3.25 In the context of the law of tort, the idea of vicarious liability is that one person may be liable for the torts of another. This kind of liability arises most frequently in the field of employment. As a preliminary, it is important to note that the law has always drawn a clear distinction between two types of relationship. First there is the relationship of master and servant, which is the rather old-fashioned terminology used to describe the straightforward relationship of an employer and an employee. Secondly, there is the relationship between an employer and an independent contractor, who is employed to do a specific task. The importance of the distinction is that generally an employer will be liable for the torts of his servants, whereas, in the main, he will not be liable for the torts of his independent contractors. This can be justified partly on the basis that an employer has more control over his own employees than he would have over independent contractors, and partly on the basis that an employer is likely to have a greater capacity to pay damages than would one of his employees.

8.3.26   Difficulties can arise in establishing whether a person is a servant or an independent contractor, but as a general guide servants are generally under the employer's control, and are integrated into his workforce and are on his payroll. For example, if a firm of window-cleaners is employed to clean library windows, they will be independent contractors, whereas if a caretaker does exactly the same thing he will be a servant. Of course, even though as between the local authority and the window-cleaning firm the latter are independent contractors, as between the firm itself and its individual window-cleaners the relationship will be one of master and servant.

8.3.27   It would be a mistake to think that the liability of a master for the torts of his servants is absolute. In fact, a master is responsible for the negligent actions of his servants only when those actions take place during the course of the servant's employment. In other words, when a servant is − to use the phrase which the courts usually employ − on a frolic of his own, the master has no liability. It seems that such a situation exists when a servant is doing something which is so unconnected with his employment that by no stretch of the imagination could it be in any way related to it. The fact, however, that the servant is doing something which is expressly forbidden by the master does not necessarily take his actions outside the scope of vicarious liability.

8.3.28   In *Harrison v. Michelin Tyre Co. Ltd.* (1985), some employees were indulging in horseplay. During the course of this the plaintiff, who was trying to work, was injured. The company were held responsible for the actions of their servants, even though such actions were expressly forbidden. The rationale behind this decision is that the employer must remain responsible for the conduct of his employees, for example, by employing supervisors.

8.3.29   In contrast, if an employee is sent from his usual work place to, for example, a meeting at some distance, he is not acting in the course of his employment if he detours to do his shopping, for he would then be on a frolic of his own.

8.3.30   Two further points must be made before leaving the topic of vicarious liability. First, there are inevitably situations where two or more people are liable for the damage caused to the plaintiff. For example, if a pedestrian is injured in a road accident caused by the negligent driving of both A and B, it would not be possible to apportion any part of the injuries to either defendant, therefore, both are liable for the whole of the pedestrian's injuries and he may choose to sue either. The defendants in this type of situation are known as concurrent tortfeasors because they are responsible for different acts of negligence which produced the same damage. Joint tortfeasors are slightly different in that they are generally people who are involved in the same act of negligence. The author, publisher and printer of a defamatory book could all be joint tortfeasors. Also, in cases of vicarious liability, the employer is a joint tortfeasor with his employee and partners in a firm are all jointly and severally liable for the torts of a partner acting in the course of the firm's business.

8.3.31 One tortfeasor may now be able to claim a contribution towards the damages awarded against him by another concurrent or joint tortfeasor. Section 1(1) of the Civil Liability (Contribution) Act 1978 provides that any person liable in respect of any damage suffered by another person may recover a contribution from any other person liable in respect of the same damage. Thus, in the previous example, if the pedestrian chooses to sue A and is awarded damages, A may take action against B for a contribution because B is some other person liable in respect of the same damage. The amount of the contribution is a matter for the discretion of the court which must consider the blameworthiness of the parties as well as the actual physical contribution made to the damage. The court can also exercise its discretion in such a way as to exempt a person from liability to make a contribution.

8.3.32 Secondly, it should be noted that when an employer is found vicariously liable to a plaintiff, he may, then, have a cause of action against the employee. This could result in an action for negligence in the courts, although in practice internal disciplinary action may be more usual.

8.3.33 Finally, from the employer's point of view, he may well have various statutory obligations to his employees. There are many statutes which impose a duty on an employer, the most comprehensive of which is the Health and Safety at Work etc. Act 1974. A breach of the duty imposed by this Act may lead to prosecutions against an employer, as non-compliance with the legislation is a criminal offence. Further, the same Act imposes a duty on employees to take reasonable care for the health and safety of fellow employees. Again, enforcement is by way of prosecution.

CONCLUSION

8.4.01 Having seen that it is possible to incur liability to the public and to employees and colleagues in a number of different circumstances, it is worth repeating that these various types of liability are not mutually exclusive, but, on the contrary, overlap and intertwine with each other.

8.4.02 It is appropriate to conclude with three specific examples to emphasize the importance of these areas of law in practice.

8.4.03 First, suppose a public library has a children's section which is heated by a gas fire, and that over the years the protective bars of the gas fire have become buckled and loose. Suppose further that very young children are often left unattended in the area whilst their parents are browsing elsewhere. Finally, suppose that a five year-old, attracted by the fire, puts his hand through the bars and is burned. These circumstances could lead to an action either under the Occupiers' Liability Act 1957, for breach of the common duty of care to visitors, or for negligence, and it is by no means unlikely that such actions would be successful.

8.4.04 Taking the same example one step further, suppose that the gas fire was in a room used by staff and the room had the word 'private' on the door. Again, if it was known that children entered the room, there could still be liability under the Occupiers' Liability Act 1984, because the three pre-conditions would apply, or again, in negligence, despite the element of trespass.

8.4.05 Thirdly, the case of *Hopkins v. Scunthorpe Corporation* (1966) [para. 8.3.12] is clearly in point.

8.4.06 Finally, at a purely practical level, the power of the court to apportion responsibility for damages in cases of vicarious liability must be remembered. If a responsible employee fails to report a potentially dangerous situation to his employer, the court could well find that the employee himself is negligent, and should take a large part − or even perhaps all − of the blame.

Appendix A

THE CITATION AND USE OF LEGAL SOURCES

Law reports

A.1.01   There are many series of Law Reports, some of which contain the full text of the court's judgment and some of which do not. It may be thought odd that a legal system which depends so heavily on the doctrine of binding precedent has no such thing as an 'official' series of reports, but this is in fact the position. The closest to 'official' series are those published by the Incorporated Council of Law Reporting for England and Wales, which is a non-profit-making body, created and run by the legal profession. Although any series of reports may be loosely referred to as 'law reports', the phrase also has a stricter meaning, namely the principal series produced by the Incorporated Council. Using the phrase in this strict sense for the moment, the *Law Reports* contain current sub-series as follows: Appeal Cases (A.C.) for House of Lords decisions; Chancery Division (Ch.); Family Division (Fam.); and Queen's Bench Division (Q.B.) covering the various divisions of the High Court and decisions of the Court of Appeal arising out of them. Oddly, in view of their title, the Law Reports also contain statutes. The topic of statutes generally is discussed in paras. A.1.07 *et seq.*

A.1.02   The Incorporated Council also publishes the *Weekly Law Reports* (W.L.R.), in three volumes each year. The cases included in volumes 2 and 3 also appear again in due course in the appropriate volume of the *Law reports*. This version is more valuable when it appears because it contains summaries of the arguments which were presented to the court, as well as the judgments, but the production of the *Weekly Law Reports* is justified by their earlier publication. However, speed is not the only advantage which the *Weekly Law Reports* have over the *Law Reports*. The *Weekly Law Reports* also provide somewhat greater coverage, since the cases reported in volume 1 of the *Weekly Law Reports* are those which the editor considers to be insufficiently important to justify the full treatment that cases receive in the *Law Reports*.

A.1.03 Unlike the products of the Incorporated Council, however, the majority of series of law reports are published as purely commercial ventures. The leading series of general law reports produced on a commercial basis is the *All England Law Reports* (All E.R.), but there are also very many specialized series, such as *Local Government Reports* (L.G.R.) and the *Justice of the Peace Reports* (abbreviated, rather oddly, simply to J.P.).

A.1.04 Several newspapers publish law reports, as do many periodicals. In the case of the latter, the reports will, naturally, relate to the periodical's subject-matter, such as the *Criminal Law Review* (Crim. L.R.) and *Local Government Review*. The value of the specialized series of free-standing reports, and of the reports incorporated into newspapers and other periodicals, is that their editors may well include cases which lack sufficient general or lasting interest to justify inclusion in the more mainstream series, and yet are of interest to specialists. However, it is important to remember that, unlike the free-standing series of reports, periodicals' reports are usually, and newspapers' reports are always, abbreviated. In other words, they are the reporter's version of what the judge said. It will be obvious, therefore, that there will always be a question-mark over the accuracy and reliability of any abbreviated report. An exception to the general proposition that reports in periodicals are abbreviated is provided by *Local Government Review*, which contains the full transcripts of the judgments.

A.1.05 The unreliability of short reports does not mean that full-transcript reports should be read uncritically. In particular it is important to distinguish between the headnote and the judgment itself. The headnote, which is the introductory summary of the decision is written by the reporter, not by the judge, and therefore it is not authoritative. The proper utility of the headnote is limited to telling the reader what the case is about, so that he can decide for himself whether it will be worth his while to invest further time and energy in reading the judgment itself.

A.1.06 In relation to case references, the distinction between square and round brackets should be noted. Where the date is in square brackets (e.g. [1988] 1 All E.R. 1), the date is an essential part of the reference, because there is a page 1 of the first volume of each year of the All England Reports since their inception in 1936. On the other hand, if the date is in round brackets (e.g. (1988) 152 J.P. 1), the date is not essential, and the volume number, together of course with the page number, would be sufficient to enable you to find the case. The round brackets method is distinctly old-fashioned and is unlikely to be encountered in current reports, except for *Justice of the Peace Reports*, Knight's *Local*

Statutes

A.1.07 The usual way of citing a statute is by its short title – for example, the Local Government Act 1972. The short title is usually found towards the end of the body of the text, but before the schedules (if any). To pursue the example of the Local Government Act 1972, the relevant provision is s. 274.

A.1.08 The convenience of being able to refer to a statute by its short title may seem to be obvious, but it becomes even clearer when the alternatives are considered.

A.1.09 First, there is the long title, which is found at the beginning of the statute. To give an indication of the unwieldy nature of the long title, it is necessary to do no more than return to the example of the Local Government Act 1972:

> An Act to make provision with respect to local government and the functions of local authorities in England and Wales; to amend Part II of the Transport Act 1968; to confer rights of appeal in respect of decisions relating to, licences under the Home Counties (Music and Dancing) Licensing Act 1926; to make further provision with respect to magistrates' courts committees; to abolish certain inferior courts of record; and for connected purposes.

A.1.10 A technical way of referring to a statute is by its year and chapter number – thus the Local Government Act 1972 may be cited as '1972, c. 70', meaning that it was the seventieth statute to receive the Royal Assent in 1972. Whilst this form of citation enables the statute to be identified, it has the clear drawback of conveying nothing of any real meaning on the face of the reference. Furthermore, this method of citation, in the form of the example which has been taken, dates only from 1962. Before that date the convention was to cite a statute according to the session of the Parliament in which it was passed, and a session of Parliament usually spans two calendar years, running from the Autumn of one year to the Summer of the next. To make matters worse, however, the session of Parliament was identified by reference to the monarch's regnal year or years, rather than the calendar years.

A.1.11 Each regnal year begins with the anniversary of the monarch's accession, which means that the present Queen's regnal year runs from February 6 of one year, to February 5 of the next. The fact that this regnal year does not correspond with the Parliamentary year causes complications because of the impossibility of foretelling the future. The difficulty is that the Queen may die or abdicate at any time, and – perhaps more probably – Parliament may be dissolved at any time. This means that where a statute was passed during the first regnal year of a session of Parliament, only that regnal year could be allocated to it, in case either the monarch or the Parliament did not survive into the next regnal year.

A.1.12 For example, the Tanganyika Independence Act 1961 is cited as 10 Eliz 2 c. 1, although in reality the session of Parliament extended into the next regnal year as well, so with the benefit of hindsight the Act could have been cited as 10 & 11 Eliz 2 c. 1. Later statutes from that session are referred to by both regnal years — e.g. the Local Government (Records) Act 1962 is 10 & 11 Eliz 2 c. 56.

A.1.13 Finally, there is the question of what is the best source for finding the actual wording of a statute. The text-book answer must be that the most authoritative version which is readily available is the text of the Queen's Printer's copy as published by Her Majesty's Stationery Office. However, in this, as in so many other things, the text-book answer overlooks a whole dimension of pure practicality. The principal deficiencies of the Queen's Printer's version are that it contains no editorial matter by way of commentary, explanation or even cross-reference, and — even more seriously — of necessity it represents the text of the Act as at the time it was passed. The Queen's Printer's version of the text is also reproduced in the *Statutes* volume of the Incorporated Council's *Law Reports*.

A.1.14 The commercially published series *Current Law Statutes Annotated* overcomes the lack of editorial matter by incorporating very full annotations, section by section, together with — in most cases — a useful introductory essay commenting on the background and purposes of the statute. The editorial process inevitably involves some delay between the Royal Assent and publication of the annotated version of the statute, but this delay is generally fairly short.

A.1.15 Perhaps the most useful version overall, however, is *Halsbury's Statutes of England*, which again is commercially published. *Halsbury's Statutes* has the advantage that the text is not only supported by full annotations, but also by an updating service which makes it relatively easy to keep track of repeals and amendments as they take place.

THE CITATION OF JUDGES' TITLES

The House of Lords

A.2.01 The Judicial Committee of the House of Lords, which is usually known simply as *the House of Lords*, consists of peers who hold, or have held, high judicial office. In practice, virtually all of them are appointed specifically to be Law Lords, or, to give them their full title, Lords of Appeal in Ordinary. Law Lords are simply referred to by their titles, e.g. *Lord Oliver*, with or without the appropriate geographical designation, which in the case of Lord Oliver is *of Aylmerton*. The Lord Chancellor, who is a member of the Government, but who can and does sit in the Judicial Committee of the House of Lords, is referred to in writing as, e.g., *Lord Mackay L.C.* As with other Law Lords, the use of the geographical designation, which in the case of Lord Mackay is *of Clashfern*, is optional.

The Court of Appeal

A.2.02 The Court of Appeal operates in two divisions, namely the Civil Division and the Criminal Division. The head of the Civil Division is the Master of the Rolls, who is referred to in writing as *Lord Donaldson M.R.* The head of the Criminal Division is the Lord Chief Justice, who is referred to in writing as *Lord Lane C.J.*, or sometimes, if somewhat tautologically, as *Lord Lane L.C.J.* Both the Master of the Rolls and the Lord Chief Justice may also sit in the High Court or the House of Lords.

A.2.03 An ordinary judge of the Court of Appeal will have the rank of Lord Justice of Appeal. This appears in writing as, e.g., *Glidewell L.J.* This form is sexually non-specific, so a female judge of the Court of Appeal will similarly appear in writing as, e.g., *Butler-Sloss L.J.* On retirement from the Court of Appeal, judges sometimes return to judicial work on a part-time basis to help out with heavy workloads. Under these circumstances they will simply be referred to, both orally and in writing, by reference to the knighthood (or damehood) which they already possessed before retirement, e.g. *Sir Denys Buckley*. Judges of the Court of Appeal may also sit in the High Court, but they will usually do so only where that court is exercising its appellate and supervisory jurisdictions.

The High Court

A.2.04 The High Court operates in three Divisions, namely the Family Division, the Chancery Division, and and the Queen's Bench Division. The head of each Division has a special title.

A.2.05 The head of the Family Division is known as the President, and is referred to in writing as, e.g., *Sir Stephen Brown P.* The effective head of the Chancery Division is known as the Vice-Chancellor, although nominally the Lord Chancellor is, of course, that Division's head. The Vice-Chancellor is referred to in writing as, e.g., *Sir Nicolas Browne-Wilkinson V-C*, or merely as *Browne-Wilkinson V-C*. The Lord Chief Justice is the head of the Queen's Bench Division of the High Court, as well as the Civil Division of the Court of Appeal.

A.2.06 Ordinary judges of the High Court, who are technically termed puisne judges (*puisne* is pronounced *puny* and merely means *junior*), are referred to in writing as, e.g., *McCullough J*. This form is sexually non-specific, so a female judge of the High Court is similarly referred to in writing as, e.g., *Booth J*.

Appendix B

PHOTOCOPYING CROWN AND PARLIAMENTARY COPYRIGHT
PUBLICATIONS

Introduction

1. This letter revises HMSO's earlier 'Dear Librarian' letter of August 1985 in the light of the Copyright, Designs & Patents Act 1988 (ISBN 0 10 544888 5, available from HMSO). It is intended to clarify the circumstances in which it is necessary to seek prior permission before photocopying Crown and Parliamentary copyright material. In recognition of the unique nature of much of this material, considerable freedom is allowed in its reproduction but within the guidance described below.

2. Under the Copyright, Designs & Patents Act 1988, a new category of 'Parliamentary copyright' was introduced. It should be noted that HMSO administers Parliamentary copyright on behalf of the House of Lords and the House of Commons in those Parliamentary works published by HMSO but Parliamentary copyright material NOT published by HMSO will be administered by officials of the relevant House of Parliament.

3. For the purposes of defining conditions for reproduction, Crown and Parliamentary copyright material can be divided into the following broad categories:

    (a) Statutory Publications, including Bills and Acts of Parliament, Statutory Rules and Orders, and Statutory Instruments;

    (b) The Official Report of the House of Lords and House of Commons Debates (Hansard), Lords' Minutes, the Vote Bundle,

Commons Order-Books and Commons Statutory Instruments Lists;

(c) Other Parliamentary papers published by HMSO, including Reports of Select Committees of both Houses;

(d) Other Parliamentary material not published by HMSO;

(e) Non-Parliamentary publications, comprising all papers of Government Departments — both published and unpublished — not contained in other categories;

(f) Charts and Navigational publications published by the MOD (Hydrographic Department) and maps and other publications in all media published by the Ordnance Survey.

4. This letter is primarily concerned with *published* Crown and Parliamentary copyright material. The photocopying of unpublished material that is subject to Crown or Parliamentary copyright may also require prior permission and unless alternative arrangements are displayed at the site where the material is held, application should be made to HMSO with regard to the Crown copyright material, at the address shown at paragraph 25, or to the appropriate House of Parliament in respect of unpublished Parliamentary copyright material, at the address shown at paragraph 26.

5. The position regarding the photocopying of published material in the six categories is set out below.

Statutory Publications (category 3(a) above)

6. There is no objection to the photocopying of extracts of up to 30% of the whole publication; it is not necessary to seek permission before doing so and no fees are levied.

7. Permission is not normally granted for the photocopying of longer extracts (i.e. of 30% or more of the whole text) or the complete text of Bills or Acts within six months of publication by HMSO. Similarly, permission is not normally granted for the photocopying of longer extracts or the complete text of Statutory Rules, Orders or Instruments within three months of publication by HMSO. Under exceptional circumstances permission may be granted within the embargo periods but formal application to HMSO is required and a fee may be levied.

8. Outside the embargo periods, these publications may be photocopied without applying for permission and no fees are levied.

The Official Reports and House business papers (category 3(b) above)

9. There is no objection to the photocopying of these publications. No fees are levied and no prior permission is required.

10 Any person or body using unofficial reports of proceedings in Parliament, even though they are photocopies of verbatim reports of speeches as reported in the Official Report, may not enjoy as extensive privilege in proceedings for defamation as the full Official Report would enjoy.

11. Reproduction from the Official Reports in connection with advertising is not permitted.

Other Parliamentary papers published by HMSO (category 3(c) above)

12. There is no objection to the photocopying of BRIEF extracts — which, for this category, may be defined as up to 5% of the whole publication; it is not necessary to seek permission before doing so and no fees are levied.

13. Permission is not normally granted for the photocopying of longer extracts (i.e. of 5% or more of the whole text) or the complete text within six months of the date of publication by HMSO. Under exceptional circumstances permission may be granted within this embargo period, but formal application to HMSO is required and a fee may be levied.

14. Outside the embargo period these publications may be photocopied without applying for permission and no fees are levied.

Parliamentary papers not published by HMSO (category 3(d) above)

15. This Parliamentary copyright material is administered by officials of the relevant House and application for its use should be made to the relevant address at paragraph 26 below.

Non-Parliamentary publications (category 3(e) above)

16. This category covers a wide range of material published by HMSO and by Government Departments and Crown bodies. Unless otherwise stated on the publication, applications are required for permission to photocopy both extracts and complete texts. A fee, calculated according to the number of pages copied, will normally be levied. The exception to this is where free Departmentally produced information publications are for any reason unobtainable, when permission for photocopying is not required. Users of such photocopies should always check on the currency of the information

in the publication.

17. Users registered by the Copyright Licensing Agency (CLA) need not apply for permission to make photocopies of material in this category providing the copying is within the terms of the CLA licence.

Charts and Navigational publications published by the MOD (Hydrographic Department) and maps and other publications in all media published by the Ordnance Survey (category 3(f) above)

18. The administration of Crown copyright relating to publications in this category is subject to appropriate arrangements for delegation between the Controller of HMSO and the MOD (Hydrographic Department) and Ordnance Survey. Application for permission to photocopy such material should be made to MOD (Hydrographic Department) or Ordnance Survey − as appropriate − at the addresses in paragraph 27.

General

19. It is not intended that the above guidance should in any way conflict with any statutory rights. In case of doubt, further clarification should be sought from HMSO at the address in paragraph 25, or, as the case may be, from the appropriate House at the address in paragraph 26.

20. Although permission is not currently required for photocopying defined classes of material in some circumstances (as detailed above), all Crown and Parliamentary rights in respect of copyright are reserved and will be asserted in cases considered by the Controller of HMSO or the appropriate House as exceptional.

21. The commercial reproduction, photocopying or microcopying of Crown and Parliamentary copyright material is not covered by this letter and is subject to separate licensing arrangements. Similarly, where it is proposed to make multiple copies or to undertake systematic or repeated copying, application must be made to HMSO or, as the case may be, to the appropriate House, unless the copying is undertaken within the terms of a licence granted by the Copyright Licensing Agency (in which case the conditions of the licence will apply), or if the copying is of material described at paragraph 22 below.

22. Multiple, systematic or repeated copying may be undertaken of the following material without seeking permission before doing so and no fees are levied:

(i) Statutory publications – extracts of up to 30% of the publication; longer extracts or the complete text if outside the embargo period (see paragraph 7).

(ii) The Official Reports and other House business papers – no restrictions, but see paragraphs 10 and 11.

(iii) Other Parliamentary papers published by HMSO – brief extracts of up to 5% of the publication.

23. Photocopies of Crown and Parliamentary copyright material in all classes are not permitted to be misused by unfair or misleading selection, undignified association or undesirable use for advertising purposes. In cases of doubt, application must be made to HMSO, or, as the case may be, to the appropriate House at the address below.

24. Librarians should be aware of Statutory Instrument 1989/1212, the Copyright (Librarians and Archivists)(Copying of Copyright Material) Regulations 1989, ISBN 0 11 0972120 and available from HMSO.

Contact

25. Unless otherwise stated above (or on the publication concerned), the address for all applications for permission to photocopy Crown and published Parliamentary copyright material – and for all enquiries about this letter – is as follows:

Her Majesty's Stationery Office
Copyright Section (P6)
St Crispins
Duke Street
NORWICH NR3 1PD

Tel: 0603 695506 (Direct Dialling)
Fax: 0603 695582

26. Enquiries regarding reproduction of Parliamentary material not published by HMSO should be directed to:

Chief Clerk	or	Clerk of the Journals
Journal Office		Journal Office
House of Lords		House of Commons
LONDON SW1A 0PW		LONDON SW1A 0AA
Tel: 071 219 3187/3327		Tel: 071 219 3315/3320

27. Other useful addresses are:

Copyright Branch
Ordnance Survey
Romsey Road
Maybush
SOUTHAMPTON SO9 4DH
Tel: 0703 792302

Hydrographic Department
Finance Section
Ministry of Defence
TAUNTON
Somerset TA1 2DN
Tel: 0823 337900 Ext 337

[Note: This letter was issued by HMSO in November 1989. The London telephone numbers have been updated to take account of the changes introduced in May 1990.]

Appendix C

CASE REFERENCES

Adam v. Ward [1916-7] All E.R. Rep. 157	3.5.12 *et seq.*
Alexander v. North Eastern Railway Co. (1865) 122 E.R. 1221	3.5.09
Anderson (W.B.) & Sons Ltd. v. Rhodes [1967] 2 All E.R. 850	1.4.24
Anns v. London Borough of Merton [1977] 2 All E.R. 492	8.3.24
Argyll v. Argyll [1965] 1 All E.R. 611	5.3.01
Associated Provincial Picture Houses Ltd. v. Wednesbury Corporation [1947] 2 All E.R. 680	2.3.17 *et seq.*
Attorney-General v. Jonathan Cape [1975] 3 All E.R. 484	5.3.02
Attorney-General v. Observer Ltd., Re an Application by Derbyshire County Council [1988] All E.R. 385	2.7.07
Attorney-General v. Smethwick Corporation [1932] All E.R. Rep. 304	2.3.09
Backhouse v. Lambeth London Borough Council [1972] *The Times*, October 14	2.3.37
Bartlett v. Sidney Marcus Ltd. [1965] 2 All E.R. 753	2.6.22
Beloff v. Pressdram Ltd. and Another [1973] 1 All E.R. 241	6.3.24
Bloodworth v. Gray (1844) 135 E.R. 140	3.3.09
Boaler v. R. (1888) 4 T.L.R. 565	3.6.05
Bognor Regis Urban District Council v. Campion [1972] 2 All E.R. 61	3.4.14
Bolton v. Stone [1951] 1 All E.R. 1078	8.3.09

Vizetelly v. Mudie's Select Library Ltd. (1900)
16 T.L.R. 352   3.5.21 *et seq.*
Wagon Mound, The (No.1) [1961] 1 All
E.R. 404   8.3.17
Wakelin v. London and S.W. Railway Co. (1866)
12 App.Cas. 41   8.3.15
Watt v. Hertfordshire County Council
[1954] 2 All E.R. 368   8.3.11
Wheat v. E. Lacon & Co. Ltd. [1966] 2 All E.R. 700   8.2.04
Weldon v. Times Book Co. Ltd. (1911)
28 T.L.R. 143   3.5.22
Whiteley v. Chappell (1868) L.R. 4 Q.B. 147   1.5.11
Youssoupoff v. Metro-Goldwyn-Mayer (1934)
50 T.L.R. 581   3.3.02; 3.4.07; 3.4.15 *et seq.*

References to *The Times* and *Shipping Gazette* are both self-explanatory.
In relation to the other series of Reports, the following key may be useful:

A.C. (and App.Cas.) = Appeal Cases
All E.R. = All England Law Reports
All E.R. Rep. = All England Law Reports Reprint (of a selection of
  cases reported before the All E.R. series began)
B & Ad. = Barnewall and Adolphus' Reports
Cox, C.C. = Cox's Criminal Cases
Cro. Jac. = Croke, Jac.
C.L.Y. = Current Law Yearbook
E.R. = English Reports
F & F = Foster and Finlason's Reports
J.P. = Justice of the Peace Reports
J.P.L. = Journal of Planning and Environment Law
L.G.R. = Local Government Reports
L.G.Rev. = Local Government Review
L.R.Q.B. = Law Reports Queen's Bench
L.T. = Law Times
Q.B. = Queen's Bench
R.P.C. = Reports of Patent, Design and Trade Mark Cases
S.L.T. = Scots Law Times
Stra. = Strange's Reports
T.L.R. = Times Law Reports
W.L.R. = Weekly Law Reports

Notes:
1 Many cases appear in more than one series of Reports, but our
tendency has been to favour the All England Law Reports on the basis

of the breadth of their availability. The various series of Reports may refer to the same case by somewhat different names. However, the variations are seldom sufficiently great to cause any real difficulty in identifying cases.

2 A case name in the form of, e.g., *The Wagon Mound* indicates that a ship was at the heart of the subject matter of the case, and the name of the ship has been adopted as the name of the case.

Index

COPYRIGHT

interpreting the law
for libraries and archives

Graham Cornish

Are databases covered by copyright? Who owns the copyright in a work? What are the justifications for fair dealing?

This book sets out in a question-and-answer fashion to explain the new UK Copyright Act and the supporting legislation. The result is a working reference tool to which librarians and archivists can turn for a ready answer. The subject index acts as a guide to the material dealt with by the questions.

Printed materials, manuscripts, audiovisual works, photographs, maps, databases, broadcasts and works of art are all covered. The law relating to copying, preservation, re-publishing, importation, exhibition and rental is examined in the context of both public and private collections.

Graham P. Cornish BA ALA MIInfSc joined the staff of the British Library in 1969. He is now Programme Office for the IFLA Universal Availability of Publications Programme, and has responsibility for copyright interpretation throughout the British Library.

216 × 138 mm; 128 pp; cased
ISBN 0-85365-709-2

VIEWPOINTS IN LIBRARY AND INFORMATION SCIENCE

This challenging series from Library Association Publishing addresses important current issues that affect every information worker. Authors who feel strongly about an issue have the opportunity to influence the debate through these pamphlets.

CHARGING FOR LIBRARY AND INFORMATION SERVICES

Bob Norton

The questions of charging and of freedom of access are complex and are often emotively expressed. Norton attempts to define the questions, and considers how, in the light of current socio-economic and user trends, a complete re-appraisal of services might be undertaken.

Bob Norton is Head of the Management Information Centre of the British Institute of Management. Having also worked as Head of Library and Information Services at the European Business Management Institute in Fontainebleau, he is also able to take a European view of information as a commodity.

210 × 148 mm; 64 pp; paper
ISBN 0-85365-818-8
Viewpoints in LIS 1

ACADEMIC LIBRARIES IN THE ENTERPRISE CULTURE

Donald Davinson

The restructured funding of universities and polytechnics encourages an entrepreneurial approach to the management of academic institutions. It provides opportunities for income generating activities, but is a potential threat to those services whose cost is not directly recoverable from the user. This pamphlet identifies the problems that managers of academic libraries may soon face and offers some solutions.

Donald Davinson BSc(Econ) DPA FLA MIInfSc worked for many years in public libraries, and was Business Librarian at Belfast City Library before pursuing an academic career at Leeds Polytechnic, where he progressed to the post of Assistant Director. He took early retirement in 1988.

210 × 148 mm; 46 pp; paper
ISBN 0-85365-579-0
Viewpoints in LIS 2

TOWARDS A UNIFIED PROFESSIONAL ORGANIZATION FOR LIBRARY AND INFORMATION SCIENCE AND SERVICES
a personal view

Wilfred L. Saunders

Emeritus Professor Saunders considers the case for bringing Aslib, the Institute of Information Scientists and The Library Association into a much closer working relationship than at present. The author advocates unification of three equal partners in order to achieve still greater internal efficiency, wider external recognition and consolidation of members' support.

Professor Saunders has expressed an idea often thought, but less often presented, to the full membership of the three organizations for consideration.

210 × 148 mm; 84 pp; paper
ISBN 0-85365-659-2
Viewpoints in LIS 3

THE WITHERING OF PUBLIC ACCESS

Trevor Haywood

A powerfully argued case for the proposition that public access to information is being impeded by the convergence of certain economic, political and technological tendencies.

Will our information needs be conveniently and cheaply networked to us, perhaps even eliminating the distinction between home and work; or will an elite of technocrats operate a closed circuit system amongst themselves, effectively exploiting an information-hungry society?

210 × 148 mm; 44 pp; paper
ISBN 0-85365-698-3
Viewpoints in LIS 4

CENSORSHIP AND LIBRARIES

Ian Malley

The regular appearance of the issue of censorship in libraries is as predictable as any problem in library management. This pamphlet examines the weakness and indecisiveness of the profession in cases of censorship. It analyses the vagueness and contradictions of censorship legislation; questions the vagaries of political interference at both local and government level; and attempts to determine whether the professional librarian in the UK is capable of assuming an effective role in a stand against censorship.

Ian Malley MA BSc is Senior Lecturer at the Department of Information Studies and Technology, Ealing College of Higher Education.

210 × 148 mm; 44 pp; paper
ISBN 0-85365-689-4
Viewpoints in LIS 5

THE MYTH OF GOVERNMENT INFORMATION

Alastair J. Allan

A discussion of recent developments in the publication of official information, concentrating on events since 1979.

A chronology outlines important changes, and three significant events are examined in detail: the changes in the role and status of HMSO, the effects of the 1979 Rayner Review on official statistics and the concept of tradeable government information ushered in by the 1983 ITAP report *Making a business of information.*

The availability of official publications for the library and the user is discussed, with a comparison between the situation in the UK and that in the USA.

The author suggests that the dissemination of government information is based largely on economic rather than social considerations.

Alastair J. Allan BLib ALA is Assistant Librarian at the University of Sheffield in charge of official publications and Chairman of the Standing Committee on Official Publications (SCOOP).

210 × 148 mm; 72 pp; paper
ISBN 0-85365-89-0
Viewpoints in LIS 6